Enhancing Teaching and Learning through Student Feedback in Medical and Health Sciences

CHANDOS
LEARNING AND TEACHING SERIES

Series Editors: Professor Chenicheri Sid Nair and Dr Patricie Mertova
(emails: sid.nair@uwa.edu.au and pmertova@hotmail.com)

This series of books is aimed at practitioners in the higher education quality arena. This includes academics, managers and leaders involved in higher education quality, as well as those involved in the design and administration of questionnaires, surveys and courses. Designed as a resource to complement the understanding of issues relating to student feedback, books in this series will respond to these issues with practical applications. If you would like a full listing of current and forthcoming titles, please visit www.chandospublishing.com.

New authors: we are always pleased to receive ideas for new titles; if you would like to write a book for Chandos, please contact Dr Glyn Jones on g.jones.2@elsevier.com or telephone +44 (0) 1865 843000.

Enhancing Teaching and Learning

Student Feedback in Medical and Health Sciences

EDITED BY
CHENICHERI SID NAIR
AND
PATRICIE MERTOVA

AMSTERDAM • BOSTON • CAMBRIDGE • HEIDELBERG • LONDON
NEW YORK • OXFORD • PARIS • SAN DIEGO
SAN FRANCISCO • SINGAPORE • SYDNEY • TOKYO
Chandos Publishing is an imprint of Elsevier

ELSEVIER

CHANDOS
PUBLISHING

Chandos Publishing
Elsevier Limited
The Boulevard
Langford Lane
Kidlington
Oxford OX5 1GB
UK
store.elsevier.com/Chandos-Publishing-/IMP_207/

Chandos Publishing is an imprint of Elsevier Limited

Tel: +44 (0) 1865 843000
Fax: +44 (0) 1865 843010
store.elsevier.com

First published in 2014

ISBN 978 1 84334 752 1 (print)
ISBN 978 1 78063 433 3 (online)

Library of Congress Control Number: 2014949974

Typeset by Domex e-Data Pvt. Ltd., India

Transferred to Digital Printing in 2014

Contents

List of figures and tables

Figures

Tables

Preface

Evaluation in higher education is aimed at reviewing whether an action or a process, particularly in the area of teaching and learning (but also other aspects of university life), has fulfilled the aims and outcomes originally envisaged. This book is the third and last in a series on utilising student feedback in disciplines and how feedback has or can be used to enhance the quality of teaching and learning in higher education. It follows on from a book entitled *Enhancing Teaching and Learning Through Student Feedback in Social Sciences*.

This volume, focussing specifically on student feedback in medical and health sciences, will provide insights into the process of evaluation and the design of evaluation within medical and health science disciplines (with a primary focus on medical education) that are currently utilised in a number of countries around the world. Most importantly, the book is aimed at showing the reader that student feedback has a place within medical and health sciences and in higher education more generally.

This volume introduces student feedback in medical and health science disciplines and draws upon international perspectives within the higher education setting. A majority of the contributors are practitioners in medical and health science disciplines and some specialise more generally in medical and health science education; however, all the chapters show contributors' perspectives on the subject and provide insights into the practices within the contributors' institutions and approaches utilised both in their higher education systems and within their particular cultural contexts.

The book is comprised of seven chapters. The first six chapters delve into the practices, views, and approaches to student feedback in higher education systems around the world. Contributions in this book come from Hong Kong, India, Thailand, Sri Lanka, the Netherlands, and Australia. The final chapter draws upon the information presented in this volume and sketches out the current trends and issues, and the future of student feedback in medical and health sciences. There is a common theme running through the majority of chapters – the value of utilising student feedback as part of quality enhancement approaches within the discipline. The main argument in this book is that such feedback is essential in improving teaching and learning strategies, the environment in which they take place, and also learning outcomes. Whilst the importance of student feedback is not disputed, it is argued in a number of cultural contexts (whether in South East Asia or the Netherlands) that the general environment often does not allow, or does not give sufficient space for, providing truly honest feedback. In this context, the authors highlight the significance of developing 'safe' learning environments, in which students feel free to provide feedback. Also evident is the infancy of the use of student feedback in many parts of the world, with the realisation that such feedback is critical in enhancing the quality of medical and health science programmes.

Chenicheri Sid Nair and Patricie Mertova

Author biographies

Chapter 1

Associate Professor Robyn Smyth is the director of learning and teaching support at the University of Southern Queensland, where she supervises teams providing professional development and student support for online, face-to-face, and blended curricula.

She has completed a doctorate investigating large-scale educational change and has leveraged that work in her practice as an academic developer working in the higher education sector for almost two decades. Her practice specialises in curriculum design in the distance and online modes, including rich media technology in higher education for student-centred pedagogies.

Robyn is an active researcher using and investigating practice, theory, and pedagogy in higher education. Her interests lie in rich media, including practice and pedagogy of m-learning, higher degree supervision, and professional development. Core research interests include using technology to support curriculum design in complex contexts, and the potential for rich media and synchronous communication tools to support student learning. Principally, her research is focussed on innovative pedagogy and managing educational change which supports innovation.

Ian Symonds is dean of the Joint Medical Program (NSW) and head of the School of Medicine and Public Health at Newcastle University. He graduated from Nottingham University in the UK and completed his postgraduate training in Obstetrics and Gynaecology in Nottingham and Birmingham. After moving to Newcastle in 2004 to take up the chair of Obstetrics and Gynaecology, he became co-chair of the curriculum implementation committee that established the JMP with the UNE. He is the censor for the Royal Australian and New Zealand College of OBGYN as well as working for the AMC in the assessment of international medical graduates.

He has edited or co-authored three undergraduate textbooks on obstetrics and gynaecology, researched and published on medical education, and holds a master's degree in clinical education.

Cathryn McCormack is a lecturer (teaching and learning) at Southern Cross University, where she supports staff in applying for teaching awards and grants, and developing their scholarship of teaching and learning.

She has been central to projects to develop student surveys at two different universities, and through these projects has developed skills and experience in qualitative and quantitative survey validation processes. Her passion lies in qualitative survey validation processes, and in particular how undertaking cognitive interviews can lead to better understanding of the basis for variation in student responses.

Her research interests are in evidence of teaching performance, situating student feedback within a larger portfolio of evidence, and how academic developers can best assist academics to reflect on the portfolio in order to improve teaching. She is currently undertaking a Ph.D investigating how academics learn to teach.

Chapter 2

Dr Julie Chen BSc, MD, FCFPC graduated from Dalhousie University, Canada, and completed her postgraduate training at the University of Toronto before becoming a fellow of the College of Family Physicians of Canada. She is currently head of undergraduate education in the Department of Family Medicine and Primary Care at the University of Hong Kong, with a joint appointment at the Institute of Medical and Health Sciences Education. In addition to teaching, she has played a leading role in the development, implementation, and evaluation of new initiatives in the medical curriculum. These include: an expanded family medicine curriculum; the 'Professionalism in Practice' programme to encourage early learning of professionalism, and a compulsory medical humanities programme which extends through all years of medical school. In recognition of her work in medical education, she was the recipient of a faculty teaching award in 2012.

Dr Weng-Yee Chin MBBS, FRACGP is a graduate of the University of Western Australia and a fellow of the Royal Australian College of General Practitioners. She worked as a private general practitioner in Sydney prior to relocating to Hong Kong in 2005. She initially joined the

Faculty of Medicine at the University of Hong Kong as an honorary family medicine teacher in 2006, and now holds joint appointments with the Department of Family Medicine and Primary Care and the Institute of Medical and Health Sciences Education, where she is primarily involved in undergraduate family medicine teaching, curriculum development, and quality assurance of the undergraduate medical curriculum. Her main research focus is in primary care mental health and in medical education.

Chapter 3

Gominda Ponnamperuma, MBBS (Colombo), Dip. Psychology (Colombo), MMEd (Dundee), Ph.D (Dundee), is a senior lecturer in medical education at the Faculty of Medicine, University of Colombo, Sri Lanka. He has published several journal articles and books, and has presented at and organised many international symposia, workshops, and conferences. He is a member of the editorial boards of two international medical education journals and has been a peer reviewer for many international journals. Gominda has been an advisor, visiting professor, and fellow of several leading academic institutes, and has also carried out consultations on educational projects in many countries around the world. He is a postgraduate tutor, examiner, and resource material developer for national and international medical education courses. His research interests include assessment (including selection for training), curriculum development, and evaluation.

Chapter 4

Cherdsak Iramaneerat is a surgeon and medical educator in Thailand. He received an MD from the Faculty of Medicine Siriraj Hospital, Mahidol University, in 1997. He enrolled in the residency training programme at the Department of Surgery, Faculty of Medicine Siriraj Hospital, and received Thai Board of Surgery in 2001. He received a scholarship from Ananda Mahidol Foundation to study medical education in the United States. He earned a master's degree in health professions education in 2004, and a Ph.D in educational psychology from the University of Illinois in Chicago in 2007. He currently works as an associate professor in the Division of General Surgery, Department of Surgery, and an associate dean in postgraduate education at the Faculty of Medicine Siriraj Hospital, Mahidol University. His work focuses on peri-operative care of surgical patients, psychology of learning, Rasch measurement, and assessment of medical students and residents.

Chapter 5

Rita Sood, MD, MMEd, FAMS, FRCP is a professor of medicine and practicing internist at the All India Institute of Medical Sciences (AIIMS), New Delhi. She has taught undergraduate and postgraduate students for more than 30 years. She has been an adjunct faculty member at the Centre for Medical Education and Technology at her institute since 1990, and headed the centre from 2005 to 2009. She has been actively involved in the faculty development programmes in medical education for the last two decades and has worked with national bodies in her country and with the WHO and UNICEF on issues concerning medical education. She has edited two books in medical education, written book chapters, published about 80 papers, and is on the review boards of many national and international journals. She was a fellow of FAIMER (Foundation for Advancement of Medical Education and Research) Institute, Philadelphia (2005–2007), and is an associate of the three regional FAIMER institutes in India. She is the President of the South-East Asian Regional Association for Medical Education (SEARAME) and the Indian Academy of Health Professions Education.

Dr Tejinder Singh MD, DNB, FIAP, MNAMS, M.Sc. HPE (Hons.) has worked at the Christian Medical College, Ludhiana, since 1986. He was appointed chair and head of paediatrics in 2006. He has been awarded fellowship by the Swedish International Development Agency, the Foundation for Advancement of International Medical Education and Research, and the Indian Academy of Paediatrics and International Medical Sciences Academy. Dr Singh has been a member of various national committees formed by the Medical Council of India and MOHFW to develop curricula for both undergraduate and postgraduate education in paediatrics. He has also contributed to the curriculum for academic development in India. Dr Tejinder Singh is the founding course director of CMCL-FAIMER Regional Institute and Medical Council of India Regional Centre for Faculty Development at Christian Medical College, Ludhiana. He has produced more than 200 other publications, including 2 books and 30 chapters.

Chapter 6

Monica van de Ridder studied educational sciences at Utrecht University and has worked in the field of medical education since 2000. Her current role is that of senior advisor for graduate, postgraduate, and continuing medical education at the Albert Schweitzer hospital (ASz) in Dordrecht, the Netherlands. The main focus of her work is quality assurance of residency training programmes, academic development (leadership in education, feedback, workplace teaching/learning, and assessment) and supervising master's degree students in educational sciences. Her special area of interest is in research on feedback in medical education, and, in particular, the link between trainees' feedback perceptions and their subsequent performance, the factors influencing the feedback process and the effect of feedback, and ways in which trainees can be encouraged to seek feedback.

Chapter 7

Sid Nair is professor of higher education at the Centre for Advancement of Teaching and Learning, University of Western Australia (UWA), Perth. Prior to this appointment, he was the quality advisor (research and evaluation) in the Centre for Higher Education Quality (CHEQ) at Monash University, Australia. He has extensive expertise in the area of quality development and evaluation, and he also has considerable editorial experience. Currently, he is associate editor of the International Journal of Quality Assurance in Engineering and Technology Education (IJQAETE). Prior to this he was also a managing editor of the Electronic Journal of Science Education (EJSE). Professor Nair is also an international consultant in a number of countries establishing quality centres, such as Oman and India. He is currently involved in a project to implement effective student evaluations across Indian universities.

Dr Patricie Mertova is currently an independent consultant with the Associates in Higher Education Policy, Development and Quality, Australia. For the past 3 years, she has been a research fellow in the Department of Education, University of Oxford, England. She was previously a research officer at the University of Queensland, and, prior to that, a research fellow at the Centre for the Advancement of Learning and Teaching (CALT) and the Centre for Higher Education Quality (CHEQ), Monash University, Australia. Her research expertise is in a broad range of education settings, including the fields of higher education, internationalisation, quality, sociology of education, adult education, educational development in law, and linguistics. She has experience in policy review and analysis. Her previous background is in the areas of linguistics, translation, cross-cultural communication, foreign languages, literature, and cultural studies.

Evaluating Student Experiences of Medical Education in the Joint Medical Programme: a Case Study of a Unique Dual University Programme

Robyn Smyth,
University of Southern Queensland

Ian Symonds,
University of Newcastle

Cathryn McCormack,
Southern Cross University

Abstract: Establishing a medical education programme in which the students are shared between two universities and regarded as a single cohort is only one complexity of an initiative begun in regional Australia in 2008. The University of Newcastle in New South Wales, which has a problem-based learning medical programme of considerable repute, partnered with the University of New England with a view to increasing understanding of rural perspectives and prompting more graduates to remain in rural locations. Assuring the quality of student outcomes was a high priority, requiring innovative approaches to devise appropriate program evaluation measures designed specifically to accommodate the unique features of the Joint Medical Programme. This chapter details the initial trials of purpose-designed instruments and methodologies and makes an initial valuation of their efficacy.

Keywords: Medical education programme; evaluation; quality assurance

Introduction

The Joint Medical Programme (JMP) is a unique initiative in the context of medical education in Australia. It is a partnership between two universities and two local health districts intended to promote training of doctors in rural settings with a view to increasing the rural doctor workforce. Two characteristics which make the JMP unique include the circumstances of each university and the regional and rural locations of these institutions, separated as they are by 400 kilometres. For more than 30 years, the University of Newcastle (UoN) has been renowned internationally for provision of a problem-based learning (PBL) approach (Henry, Byrne, & Engel, 1997) to medical education and is located in a large regional centre serviced by several major teaching hospitals. The University of New England (UNE) is a regional university renowned for its distance learning courses, and is located in a small highland rural city midway between Sydney and Brisbane. It has access to one large regional base hospital, several rural referral hospitals, and a range of small community hospitals.

The JMP cohort of students is a shared cohort, split 110:60 between UoN and UNE, with opportunities provided for all students to move between the two primary locations and five clinical schools during their training. In particular, students must undertake a minimum of four weeks of rural clinical placements and may spend up to a year in a rural area during the final two years of their training. These clinical placements are located across northern areas and the central coast of New South Wales. They provide a range and variety of rural and regional settings in which students are able to experience the diversity of primary, rural, referral, and tertiary medicine.

As part of its registration with the Australian Medical Council (AMC), the governing body for medical education, the JMP is regarded as a single entity delivering a single programme. Delivering such a programme, where two separate universities collaborate to deliver approved student outcomes in the context described above, makes the JMP a unique and particularly complex enterprise. From student management, teaching, learning, and evaluation perspectives, an enormous effort has been directed at achieving equity and coherence, since pre-existing student management and teaching and learning systems at both institutions were not interoperable, and the distance between UoN and UNE required duplication of most administrative and many teaching functions. New processes were devised for cohort management for all aspects of the JMP, from admission to learning management systems, video-conferencing, examination supervision and handling, teacher evaluation, peer review, course/programme quality assurance, and ongoing evaluation. Where possible, established practices were adopted or adapted. For example, admission procedures retained established interview practices with innovation continuing to inform selection (Hurwitz, Kelly, Powis, Lewin, & Smyth, in press). Additionally, the nature of academic staff appointments resulted in the trialling of many new or amended approaches and processes. Other than core academic appointments, these were a mix of sessional and casual contracts, fixed term appointments, and many guest lecturers drawn on a voluntary basis from a pool of local practitioners in an effort to embed rural perspectives. This mix presented opportunities to expand online learning and technology use to support student engagement and maximise efficiency.

In terms of approaches to teaching and learning, the Newcastle PBL model was adopted, with the addition of joint lectures via videoconferencing. Lecturers were invited to trial lecture capture, videoconference recording, personal response systems in lectures, new ways of structuring lectures, and other innovations. Lecturers were also provided with professional development resources to assist preparation of presentations and structure of teaching. PBL tutors in both locations were recruited from among available general practitioners, relevant sciences academics, and others; all received tutor training in PBL and were mentored during their initial semesters. Each of these activities was intended to improve student outcomes, and so students were asked for formative and summative evaluation (Biggs, 1991). The UNE students voluntarily undertook to provide additional feedback on lectures through the efforts of the UNE Medical Students Association, which initiated focus group discussions about improvement (Fraser, Smyth, Walker, & Whitfield, 2010, 2011).

The subject of this chapter is the approach devised to evaluate learning and teaching in this PBL programme, gathering consistent data across the whole cohort. Although each university had established mechanisms for collecting students' feedback on teachers and courses, these only sampled those students enrolled at each respective university and were not always well suited to evaluating teaching in the medical setting. Hence, there was a need to develop a new set of instruments administered across all JMP students and unique to that programme. The challenges outlined briefly above made traditional course and teacher evaluation ineffectual because cohort data was required, particularly in relation to learning in a PBL curriculum where one tutor usually works intensively with eight students for six hours per week in the tutorial setting.

Evaluating the learning experience in the JMP: initial cohort 2008-2011

As Daniel Stufflebeam and others remind us, programme evaluation is the 'assessment of any co-ordinated set of activities directed at achieving goals' (Stufflebeam & Shinkfield, 2007, 136). The intent of the evaluative schema for the JMP is curriculum improvement, to the benefit of student learning outcomes. The theoretical basis of the JMP schema is Stufflebeam's Context Input Product and Process (CIPP) model (Stufflebeam, 1988) and incorporates later thinking, which confirmed that evaluation should 'decide whether a given programme ... is worth continuing, repeating, modifying or extending' (Stufflebeam & Shinkfield, 2007, 346). These were the basic intentions guiding the creation of the JMP as evaluative processes were developed and formative and summative instruments were trialled.

The primary evaluative methodology chosen at programme commencement in 2008 was based on continuous improvement cycles, because both universities were using similar approaches to curriculum and business improvement. The combination of a conceptual framework from the CIPP model with a continuous improvement approach is quite a powerful marriage, which is sensible in this context since it enables thoughtful accountability (Padró, 2005). As the primary purpose was to facilitate improvement, the evaluative schema needed to fulfil basic conditions for effective quality assurance and, for best results, to focus on outcomes rather than inputs alone (Latchem, 2012, 15; Stufflebeam & Shinkfield, 2007, 23). Principally, the approach was formative and needed to be purposeful and straightforward, coherent and appropriate for its context, and to provide meaningful outcomes which would serve the students well and achieve institutional goals for quality improvement (Stufflebeam, 1988; Stufflebeam & Shinkfield, 2007, 25). As Padró reminds us:

> When used to drive planning and generate improvement through participation, feedback and evaluation, CIP (continuous improvement process) provides an opportunity to document how institutional activities comply with planned arrangements (Padró, 2005, 54, parentheses added).

The review cycle was based on a five-year time span comprising five phases consistent with both UoN and UNE evaluation frameworks:

initiate, implement, monitor, review, and report. This time-span was also congruent with the length of a five-year degree programme and generally aligned to AMC accreditations, which are between five and ten years apart. Each course within the degree programme would be reviewed in its year cluster every five years according to an agreed calendar (as shown in the sample in Table 1.1). The evaluation framework commenced operation with Year 1 in 2008.

As described below, the schema met reasonableness (Stufflebeam, 1988) criteria and also yielded useful data which formed the basis of professional development, structural adjustments, and other efforts intended to improve teaching and learning experiences for students.

The analysis described here is confined to the first three years of the JMP programme, since these are the years where the curriculum is taught primarily at either university using the established Newcastle PBL model. The intent was to use evaluation formatively to improve practice, as well as summatively to assure quality and meet institutional expectations for data which could be reported to government as part of its requirements to sustain funding on an ongoing basis. As years four and five are taught in clinical settings where the PBL model varies slightly, according to the clinical rotation of smaller groups of students spread across five clinical schools, data collection was less straight-forward. Nonetheless, the primary *Learning Experience (LEX) Questionnaires* were developed to enable ongoing capture of relevant data.

Governance of a medical programme is a critical factor for effectiveness of quality assurance. In this case, quality assurance was the responsibility of the Monitoring and Evaluation Committee (MEC), which reported directly to the JMP Committee, the ultimate governing board for the

Table 1.1   Sample from the evaluation planning calendar

	Year 1	Year 2	Year 3	Year 4	Year 5	All Years
2008	Implement	*Initiate*				
2009	Monitor	Implement	*Initiate*			
2010	Monitor	Monitor	Implement	*Initiate*		
2011	Review	Monitor	Monitor	Implement	*Initiate*	
2012	*Initiate*	Review	Monitor	Monitor	Implement	
2013	Implement	*Initiate*	Review	Monitor	Monitor	
2014	Monitor	Implement	*Initiate*	Review	Monitor	Accreditation Report

programme. The MEC oversaw the survey processes, and provided data to year committees (teaching teams), which was used to inform curriculum decisions for succeeding cohorts and to close the loop with students by providing information about how courses had been altered following their feedback. As a quality assurance measure, common instruments and processes were applied to cohorts on both campuses simultaneously, necessitating the move to online data gathering. MEC membership consisted of the academic developer chairs of year committees, the evaluation officer, student representatives from each university, the JMP executive officer, and the chair of the JMP Committee.

The primary evaluation processes developed to satisfy the needs described above are shown below in Figure 1.1. This flow chart shows the roles of the core stakeholders with responsibility for programme improvement. The Monitoring and Evaluation Committee held oversight for the development, refinement and administration of student feedback instruments and processes. This committee reported to the overall programme governance committee, the JMP Committee which directed course co-ordinators through the year committees to plan, enact, monitor and re-evaluate desired improvements. Within each evaluation cycle, there were opportunities for reflection and monitoring, with teaching and administrative staff providing input in readiness for the next cycle. Core questions remained stable but there was provision to add questions, particularly to capture information about changes made in response to the previous cohort's feedback. Process changes were documented in the semester reports and routinely discussed at MEC meetings where the evaluation team presented data and discussed outcomes and trends as they developed.

Both formative and summative data were required in order to evaluate student experiences responsively within the PBL approach to curriculum implementation, and to capture episodes and elements of interaction and teaching, as well as the means of assessing learning within the curriculum (Stake & Tineke, 2001; Stufflebeam & Shinkfield, 2007). This intent led to the choice of a mixed method approach to gather rich data for specific purposes alongside routine and institutional quantitative data. As a further assurance of rigour, the survey schema was approved by the Human Ethics Research Committee of each university prior to implementation. The ultimate governing board for the programme ensured transparency and enabled further opportunities for the approach and processes to be scrutinised and suggestions for improvement made through annual reporting to the JMP Committee.

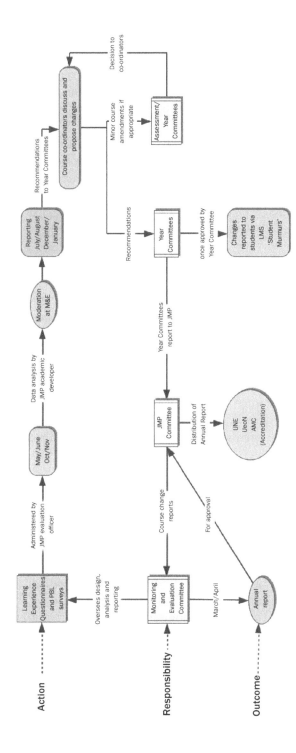

Action - - - - - - - - - -

Responsibility - - - -

Outcome - - - - - - - -

Figure 1.1 Process Chart for the Joint Medical Programme student Evaluation of Courses Process

The instruments, their purpose and reflection on performance

The approach to and set-up for evaluation in this unique context made data collection fraught, because institutional evaluations of teacher performance were inconsistent, the accrediting body required cohort data, and the intense nature of PBL programmes meant that teacher evaluation was quite problematic. Therefore, a mixed-method approach based on a quality improvement paradigm, formative and summative qualitative data, trial of collegiate peer review, and student-led evaluation of lectures (Fraser, et al., 2010, 2011) were all combined to provide useful evidence for improving practice.

For example, in 2008, the first year of the programme, a PBL tutor survey was undertaken mid-semester with the intent of providing formative feedback for tutors. After six weeks of working with the tutor six hours per week in a small group of eight students, some students reported that they felt anonymity could not be guaranteed and that they could face repercussions for the rest of the semester if they provided negative feedback. Tutors felt similarly uncomfortable in receiving feedback, both positive and negative, within the context of the close relationships that had developed. As a result, individual tutor surveys were discarded and replaced with a two-phased approach of peer mentoring (Smyth, Horton, Outram, & Bossu, 2008) alongside the more general approach to collecting student feedback discussed below.

Qualitative instruments

A series of formative and summative instruments were designed to capture a range of data concerning student experience and to be used as a cumulative indicator to guide improvement in practice.

Briefly, the primary formative instruments consisted of three short qualitative surveys designed to monitor students' experiences of learning through the PBL approach. These were:

A. Getting Started in PBL (applied mid-semester one of year one to evaluate commencing experiences)

1. What have you valued most about the Problem Based Learning (PBL) approach?

2. What has been challenging about learning using the PBL approach?

3. What could we improve to assist your learning using the PBL process?

4. So that we can help next year's commencing students better, please tell us how we can improve on the support provided to you this year.

Biographical data gathering was common to all surveys:

5. About you:

I am studying at: ☐ University of Newcastle ☐ University of New England

I was: ☐ Admitted as part of the Rural and Remote Admissions Scheme

I am an:

☐ Aboriginal/Torres Strait Islander

☐ International student

I am: ☐ Male ☐ Female

B. Continuing in PBL (applied semester two of Year 2 to evaluate three semesters of experience)

1. Please select three or four words from the following list that describe your PBL experience.

2. Describe how you learn using the Problem Based Learning (PBL) approach?

3. What do you think you are meant to be achieving in the closing tutorials?

4. If you were a PBL tutor, describe how you would run your PBL tutorials.

C. Remote PBL (applied in semesters one and two of Year 3 to evaluate the use of videoconferencing technology as a means of remote attendance at PBL tutorials while students were on clinical rotation).

1. Please select three or four words from the following list that describe your PBL experience.

2. How did you find working with your PBL group from a remote location using technology?

3. What difficulties and frustrations have you encountered?

4. If you were a PBL tutor, describe how you would run your remote PBL tutorials.

In addition, clinical experience surveys were applied in clinical rotations in both semesters in the third year to evaluate experience in clinical settings.

The rich data gathered formatively enabled rapid responses to issues such as timing of assessment, the desire of students to have lectures captured and available online, or minor procedural inconsistencies. For example, students often indicated impatience if there was a delay in making lectures available online, despite the requirements for 80 per cent attendance at lectures, as they wanted to revisit them for revision and consolidation of learning. Student expectations about the form, frequency, and depth of feedback appeared as the strongest trend in the first three years, so new initiatives designed to enable more timely feedback on formative assessment were initiated. Similarly, student concern about duplication and variety of examination questions in Year 2 prompted a question-mapping analysis, the outcomes of which were provided to students and staff so that decisions could be made as transparently as possible.

The summative data gathering instrument was the Learning Experience Questionnaire (LEX), comprising qualitative and quantitative data gathering and administered each semester to all students in years 1–3. These surveys comprised core common questions for each course and year as well as optional and additional questions as required by teaching teams. The core questions were:

LEX Core Questions

1. **Overall I would rate MEDI1000 as:**
   Consider how the FRSs supported the working problems, how well they co-ordinated with practical sessions, and how much you learnt.

2. **The best aspects of MEDI1000 were: (qualitative)**
   Comments: *e.g. What helped you learn the most? What were the most enjoyable learning experiences you had?*

3. **The things most in need of improvement in MEDI1000 were: (qualitative)**
   Comments: *e.g. What were you asked to do that you felt was a waste of time? What things were confusing and difficult to sort out? What were the least enjoyable learning experiences you had?*

4. **I understood what I needed to do to be successful in this unit**
   Success could be achieving a particular grade on assessment tasks, completing learning activities, or achieving your personal learning goals.
   Comments: *e.g. How could study demands and assessment requirements be communicated more clearly and effectively?*

5. **I found the learning activities helpful**
   Learning activities are anything for which marks were NOT allocated. These might include lectures, tutorials, laboratory sessions, intensive school, fieldwork, clinical placement, reflective questions, and discussion board participation.
   Comments: *e.g. Which of the activities were the most interesting and helpful to your learning? Why? Which were the least? Why? How effectively was the purpose of the activities communicated to you?*

6. **The assessment tasks allowed me to demonstrate what I learned**
   Assessment tasks are anything you were asked to do for which a S/NS grade or marks were allocated.
   Comments: *e.g. Which assessment tasks were the most interesting and helpful to your learning? Why? How could you demonstrate what you learned?*

7. **I found the assessment feedback helpful**
   Assessment feedback refers to all comments about your assignments.
   Comments: *e.g. How useful was the feedback in helping you improve on your next assessment task? If it wasn't helpful, why wasn't it helpful? How could it have been more helpful? What time frame were you expecting it to be returned in?*

8. **The resources associated with this unit contributed to my learning**
   Resources may include any textbook, handouts, study guide, CD-ROM, WebCT materials and discussion board, audio or video recordings, e-reserve, or other library resources.
   Comments: *e.g. What were the most useful resources? How could the resources overall be improved?*

9. **How many hours per week did you spend working on MEDI1000**
   Include all time spent on learning activities such as class time (lectures, tutorials, laboratory sessions), reading, reflecting, online, doing assignments, private study, field trips, and intensive schools
   Comments: *e.g. What activities took the bulk of your time? How effectively was your time spent in the unit?*

10. **I feel the amount of work I was required to do was appropriate**
    Comments: *e.g. Where do you feel time was well spent, and where was time spent inefficiently?*

The things (max 3) that I would recommend for MEDI1000 are:

Change nothing – it was great!

Make other units more like this one

Improve the sequence of learning

Present material more clearly

Provide opportunities for practice without penalty

Include a greater variety of assessment tasks

Make lectures more interactive

Organise more interesting online discussions

Other:

Trend data confirmed anecdotal and formative data, which showed high rates of student satisfaction as well as providing ample opportunity for students to provide critique. In the main, students were positive in complaint and made suggestions which were reasonable and often feasible to implement quite quickly. Despite favourable opinions, response rates were lower than hoped, ranging from 28–32 per cent despite the use of numerous strategies to clarify the purpose of LEX as the basis of continuous improvement. Routine university evaluations added to student evaluation burden, being used to generate data related to government provision of programme funding.

The LEX evaluation measures were all delivered online and provided deep, rich data, which was analysed with the assistance of the NVivo data management programme. In particular, the cueing questions associated with each LEX rating question resulted in detailed and relevant student comments. These cueing questions were based on common probing questions used when undertaking cognitive interview validation (Willis, 2005) of the instrument at UNE in 2006 (McCormack, 2008).

Each semester, a report was prepared for each survey and accumulated for each year committee (teaching team) to examine and use for curriculum improvement. These reports were also intended to guide overall planning for improvement. Subsequent improvement plans were communicated between year committees and the MEC. Finally, an annual report was produced each year, providing an overall view of areas of strength and areas in need of improvement, based on trends and cross case analysis. The strength of the annual report arose from the cumulative cross-survey multi-cohort analysis which distilled common strengths and areas for improvement as well as trends and progress against desired improvements. By Year 3, trend data was enabling reflection on improvements and how well these improvements had progressed. These reports became part of the routine reporting to governance committees and against accreditation of the programme.

Reflections on performance, years 1–3

The excerpt below from the executive summary of the 2011 Annual Report shows the emphasis and style, as well as the results from the analysis of data over the six semesters since programme inception:

For all courses in 2011, student feedback was very positive with in excess of 95 per cent of respondents reporting their overall satisfaction as *good, very good* or *excellent* in years 1 and 2. In general, respondents' suggestions for improvement were thoughtful and mostly practical.

The most common area for improvement across courses in the programme is the provision of more formative feedback, especially on assessment tasks. This latter issue is being considered by the Assessment Committee and underpinned projects such as the trial of the Personal Response System in year 2. Here a positive correlation was found in student performance when MCQs were used as formative feedback tools in FRS/lecture sessions.

Evidence of change since previous offerings of courses

Data analysis for 2011 shows some evidence that recommendations made in 2009/10 are being acted upon. For example:

- assessment tasks are generally now regarded as providing positive evidence of learning.
- the FRS review has resulted in recommendations to lecturers about design and content of lectures being accepted and implemented. Hence less negative comment in student evaluation about lack of interactivity.
- although the use of the Elluminate software has been piloted for remote PBL in Year 3 with some success in enabling students to interact with their PBL groups whilst on placement, data indicates that its impact on learning should be more rigorously investigated.

Suggestions for Improving Evaluation

In the short surveys intended to focus on PBL, it may be useful to add an item to the biographical data collection which allows respondents to indicate whether they are school leaver or mature aged entrants. This will enable further dissection of the data, should it be needed.

Given the impending curriculum change, consideration could be given to trialling other evaluation measures and approaches, perhaps with a more student-focussed intention.

The data from the LEX fulfilled its purpose of providing a coherent dataset over time, as well as guiding continuous improvement as the programme evolved. In addition to this formal evaluation regime, students at the UNE campus initiated a student review of lectures in the first semester of each year, which provided additional data to be used for improvement through the provision of professional development or related resources (Fraser, et al., 2010, 2011). This data was most useful for commencing the development of online resources for sessional lecturers to improve their teaching styles. One of the issues for the JMP, like other medical schools, has been that many sessional lecturers generously volunteer their time to pass on their significant practical knowledge and experience and so formal professional development programmes do not always suit their needs. Instead, self-paced or purely informational resources began to be developed for online delivery by the academic developer and colleagues so that staff and students could access them easily.

Closing the loop for students

Student-centred approaches to data gathering were piloted on several occasions for formative surveys in order to introduce variety and to determine whether there were less formal or traditional ways of gathering targeted feedback. One approach which proved successful was the use of a list of terms, from which students chose three which best described the issue under scrutiny. These were then translated into word wheels which represented student opinion effectively, as shown in Figure 1.2 below. The lists of terms were devised to include an equal distribution of positive and negative terms as well as a few neutral terms. The resulting wheels were constructed to display the terms from greatest to least frequency, and these typically showed a firm direction towards the positive or negative. This data was then compared to results from the analysis of corresponding LEX surveys for triangulation, and also to gauge overall strength of student voice. In the example below, students commented on the use of technology for remote attendance at PBL tutorials in Year 3, when clinical rotations make it difficult to return to campus.

Students were well aware that their insight was being used to stimulate improvement, and this encouraged ongoing engagement with the feedback processes. Response rates to formative measures were

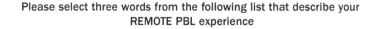

Please select three words from the following list that describe your
REMOTE PBL experience

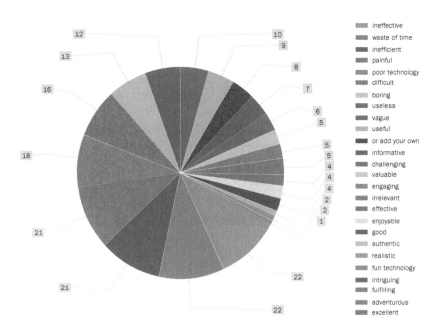

Figure 1.2 Data Sample from word association item Year 3 Remote PBL Survey

reasonable, mostly in the range of 28–35 per cent, although further efforts are underway to ensure that students realise the extent to which their reflections informed change. These include more explicit communications with students across multiple channels and through student representatives on MEC and with student consultative committees.

Issues of dependability, credibility, and trustworthiness

Like most researchers, the evaluator's task is to establish the trustworthiness of the data, providing sufficient evidence to establish that the approach is appropriate, comprehensive, and significant. This can be done by establishing conditions that ensure:

1. data collection strategies are well chosen, contextually appropriate (given any constraints such as time and cost), comprehensive, and capable of generating legitimate results;

2. data analysis is well articulated, appropriate, and auditable;

3. interpretations are well grounded in the data, feasible, consistent without excluding plausible discrepancies (Goetz & LeCompte, 1982; 1984).

Since the JMP approach included instruments designed specifically to suit the programme context, used recognised data management software to establish its audit trails, and presented data which included the unexpected, the approach demonstrated core elements of trustworthiness (Denzin & Lincoln, 2008).

Attempts to establish the three conditions above must rely on establishing that the output of an evaluation reflects the contexts of all stakeholders, so that confirmability is achieved and credibility, dependability, and transferability are established (Guba & Lincoln, 1989). In the JMP evaluation schema,

1. credibility (internal validity and reliability), was established by ensuring that the evaluator had experience of immersion in the environment, which provided contextual richness as a basis for checking, questioning, and theorising;

2. confirmability (objectivity) and dependability (external reliability), were demonstrated by acknowledging personal assumptions, beliefs and attitudes, defining an audit trail and returning results to year committees to confirm interpretations as evaluation proceeded;

3. transferability (external validity), was tested by scrutinising the analysis for specific contextualised occurrences in which data from various sources was convergent or divergent and assessing the generalisability of the process (Miles & Huberman, 1994).

In the initial implementation period, accreditation reviews by the AMC complemented the JMP on its student experience data, the outcomes of which also aligned well with independent student analysis of lectures. Trend analysis at the end of 2011 indicated that the evaluation outputs were useful indicators or areas for improvement which were confirmed by other data such as teacher reflection.

Conclusions

The JMP is a unique medical programme involving two universities collaborating to deliver a single programme dispersed over a large area of rural and regional northern New South Wales, Australia. Managing student administration and learning was complex, thus purposefully designed evaluation instruments were developed to implement quality monitoring cycles. This has helped gather deep, rich data on student experiences which has prompted effort to improve consistency and coherence of student learning. Overall, 90–95 per cent of students consistently rated their satisfaction with their learning experiences in positive terms. The evidence generated by the evaluation schema has met criteria for trustworthiness and generated useful data to inform quality improvement cycles.

References

Biggs, J. (Ed) (1991). *Teaching for Learning: the View from Cognitive Psychology*. Hawthorn, Vic: Australian Council for Educational Research.

Denzin, N. K., & Lincoln, Y. S. (Eds) (2008). *Collecting and Interpreting Qualitative Materials* (Third ed.). Thousand Oaks: Sage.

Fraser, J., Smyth, R., Walker, R., & Whitfield, A. (2010). *Student critical appraisal of rural medical school's fixed resource sessions*. Paper presented at the ANZAME: The Association for Health Professional Education Conference 2010, James Cook University, Townsville.

Fraser, J., Smyth, R., Walker, R., & Whitfield, A. (2011). *Rural students get down and dirty in curriculum grass*. Paper presented at the ANZAHPE 2011: LOCAL? GLOBAL? Health Professional Education for Social Accountability, Alice Springs.

Henry, R., Byrne, K., & Engel, C. (Eds) (1997). *Imperatives in Medical Education: The Newcastle Approach*. Newcastle: The Faculty of Medicine and Health Sciences, University of Newcastle.

Hurwitz, S. B., Kelly, B., Powis, D., Lewin, T., & Smyth, R. (in press). *The desirable qualities of future doctors*. Medical Teacher.

Latchem, C. (2012). *Quality Assurance Toolkit for Open and Distance Non-formal Education*. Vancouver, Canada: Commonwealth of Learning.

McCormack, C. (2008, October 2–3). *Motivation: an appropriate topic for a teaching evaluation?* Paper presented at the AHEEF, Melbourne.

Padró, F. F. (2005, 28–29th November). *Using continuous improvement process as a means of evaluating and documenting institutional performance*. Paper presented at the Evaluation Forum 2005, University Learning And Teaching: Evaluating And Enhancing The Experience, University of New South Wales, Australia.

Smyth, R., Horton, G., Outram, S., & Bossu, C. (2008). *Peer review of teaching in the context of a problem-based curriculum*. Paper presented at the Centre for Teaching and Learning: Peer Review of Staff Projects, University of Newcastle.

Stake, R. E., & Tineke, A. A. (2001). Stake's responsive evaluation: core ideas and evolution. *New Directions for Evaluation, 92* (Winter), 7–21.

Stufflebeam, D. L. (1988). The CIPP model for program evaluation. In G. F. Madaus, M. S. Scriven, & D. L. Stufflebeam (Eds.), *Evaluation Models: Viewpoints on Educational and Human Services Evaluation* (pp. 117–142). Boston: Kluwer-Nijhoff Publishing.

Stufflebeam, D. L., & Shinkfield, A. J. (2007). *Evaluation Theory, Models, and Applications*. San Francisco: Jossey Bass.

Willis, G. B. (2005). *Cognitive Interviewing: A Tool for Improving Questionnaire Design*. Thousand Oaks: Sage Publications Inc.

Acknowledgements

Many staff of the JMP contributed to the conceptualisation and refinement of the evaluation approach and instruments and although they are unnamed, their contributions are appreciated.

Using Student Feedback to Enhance Teaching and Learning in an Undergraduate Medical Curriculum: the University of Hong Kong Experience

Julie Y Chen & Weng Yee Chin,
Li KaShing Faculty of Medicine, University of Hong Kong

Abstract: The undergraduate medical curriculum at the University of Hong Kong incorporates a diverse range of teaching and learning approaches to enable students to acquire the knowledge and to develop the skills and attitudes necessary to become doctors. To help enhance and assure the quality of the wide array of educational approaches used across the curriculum, student feedback has been built into the curriculum. The importance of giving feedback to students and receiving feedback from them at an individual level as well as at a program level is recognised, with a primary focus on improving learning and teaching. Feedback is also essential in monitoring the student learning experience, which is an important factor in shaping both academic and personal development. This feedback is collected through standardised evaluation forms, regular staff-student consultative meetings, interim structured and ad hoc progress meetings with individual students, in-class quizzes, and as part of reflective writing assignments. The usefulness of, and difficulties with, student feedback in the University of Hong Kong setting will be discussed here, beginning with case examples from disciplinary and modular contexts and then taking broader program- and university-wide perspectives.

Keywords: Student feedback; medical curriculum; undergraduate; family medicine; Hong Kong

Introduction

Overview of the medical curriculum at the University of Hong Kong

The Bachelor of Medicine, Bachelor of Surgery (MBBS) program at the University of Hong Kong (HKU) is an undergraduate degree program which enables graduates to register as licenced medical doctors in Hong Kong. The goal of the six-year medical curriculum is to produce 'doctors with demonstrated competence in the understanding and delivery of effective, humane and ethical medical care who are committed to lifelong learning and are ready to proceed to postgraduate training' (The 6-Year Medical Curriculum Handbook, 2012).

To achieve this, the core content of the curriculum focuses on learning about the human body in health and disease, professional skills (problem solving, interpersonal communication, and management), population health and services, and medical ethics and professionalism. In the earlier years, a small group problem-based learning (PBL) approach predominates. Learning is structured around clinical cases which encourage students to take the lead in identifying and determining how to explore key issues triggered by the case. This approach is supplemented with traditional lecture-based teaching which complements and enhances the content of the PBL cases. In the later clerkship years, experiential learning, with small group bedside clinical teaching in hospital and community-based attachments, in a variety of clinical disciplines, comprises the bulk of student learning. New initiatives focusing on the medical humanities and professionalism are also woven into the core curriculum, both through a series of workshops and through hands-on practice.

Learning is organised into body system blocks in the initial years of training, and then into clinical disciplinary blocks in the later years, as students rotate through the various clinical specialties (Figure 2.1). Because of this, there are numerous teachers involved in each block or rotation, with each teacher usually responsible for one or two lectures of the 50 in a given block, or one or two teaching sessions within the dozens of teaching sessions which take place in a clinical rotation. Teachers usually only have sustained contact with students during the small group PBL learning, in which one teacher will work with the same small group of students for the duration of a block. With a complex curriculum that involves hundreds of university-based as well as community-based teachers, the monitoring and enhancement of teaching and learning requires both an individual and a centrally co-ordinated effort to be effective.

Year 1:

Introduction to the Art and Sciences of Medicine

Core University English (6 credits)	Mid-term Formative Exam	Introduction to the Art and Sciences of Medicine	Term Break for Revision	Summative Exam	CCC (if courses are available in the summer semester)
2-4 Common Core Courses (12-24 credits)	Term Break for Semester 1	2-4 Common Core Courses (12-24 credits)			

Sep   Mid Apr   May   Jun   Aug

Year 2:

RESP System	CVS System	URO System	Term Break for Semester 1	GI System	MSS System	Term Break for Revision	Summative Exam	CCC (if courses are available in the summer semester)
1-2 Common Core Courses (6-12 credits)				1-2 Common Core Courses (6-12 credits)				

Sep   Early Dec   Early Jan   April   Late May   Jun   Aug

Year 3:

CNS System	H & N System	HI System	Term Break for Semester 1	ENDO System	Term Break for Revision	Summative Exam	Integrated Block (A)	Elective
Practical Chinese for MBBS Students (6 credits)								

Sep   Early Dec   Early Jan   Early Feb   Early Mar   End Jan

Year 4:

Integrated Block (B)	Formative Exam	Junior Clerkship Medicine Block	Junior Clerkship Surgery Block	Junior Clerkship Multidisciplinary Block	Term Break for Revision	Summative Exam
English for Clinical Clerkships (6 credits)						

Aug   Mid Oct   Jan   Mid Apr   May

Year 5:

Senior Clerkship Medicine Block	Senior Clerkship Surgery Block	Senior Clerkship Multidisciplinary Block	Specialty Clerkship Medicine Block	Specialty Clerkship Obstetrics & Gynaecology Block	Specialty Clerkship Orthopaedics & Traumatology/ Emergency Medicine Block

Jul   Jan   Jun

Year 6:

Specialty Clerkship Paediatrics & Adolescent Medicine Block	Specialty Clerkship Psychiatry & Family Medicine Block	Specialty Clerkship Surgery Block	Revision Sessions	Final Exam	Elective	Pre-internship Block

Jul   Jan   Mar   Mid Apr   Jun

Figure 2.1 HKU MBBS Curriculum Structure

Role of feedback in medical education at HKU

Student feedback is a critical aspect of medical education and has been an area of focus discussed in the key textbooks geared towards teachers involved in medical education (Dent & Harden, 2009; Dornan, Mann, Scherpbier, & Spencer, 2011). It is the cornerstone of an effective quality assurance system in higher education (Nair & Mertova, 2011) and is used extensively at this institution at both the individual and systemic levels.

Although teaching and learning quality may be enhanced through a variety of means, this chapter focuses specifically on the role of feedback given to and received from students in the context of undergraduate medical education at HKU. In this setting, feedback is considered to be a formative process, intended to help the recipient to improve, whether the student, the teacher, or the curriculum as a whole. Only one feedback mechanism, the Student Evaluation of Teaching and Learning (SETL) questionnaire, is automatically included as a formal means of evaluating teaching quality during an individual teacher's annual performance review.

Feedback given to students may come from teachers, but may also be from peers, other faculty members, or from patients in order to monitor progress, identify gaps in learning, and to address concerns about academic progress. Individual teachers and program co-ordinators may also solicit feedback on teaching and the curriculum from students. The purpose of the feedback may be to confirm achievement of desired learning outcomes, satisfaction with the content and teaching approach, or to seek advice on new teaching initiatives. The timing of providing feedback or obtaining feedback is dependent on the specific aim.

Feedback to and from students in medical education settings

Feedback in large-class settings

In the junior years, lectures occupy about 20–30 per cent of teaching and learning time in the HKU MBBS curriculum. They can be an effective tool in conveying and explaining information, but large class sizes of over 200 can make it difficult to gauge students' understanding of material covered in the lecture and subsequently to provide timely intervention if necessary. Some interactive techniques such as a brief multiple choice questionnaire (MCQ) are useful for allowing the lecturer to obtain feedback on student understanding of the material or concepts being taught (Brown & Manogue, 2001). With an audience response system, or 'clicker' technology, this can be done more efficiently and allow for immediate anonymous feedback (Cain, Black, & Rohr, 2009). The instructor can ask questions through visual presentation software and students use their remote input devices to respond to the questions.

Example: HKU iClass

A novel system was recently developed at HKU which enabled students to use their own mobile device (smartphone or tablet) or laptop computer for this purpose in the lecture theatre. Since such devices are ubiquitous among students at present, they simply downloaded the free iClass app (compatible with both iphone and Android platforms and also Apple or PC) and were able to engage with the instructor during the lecture (Fok, 2012). During a series of whole-class lectures, the authors used iClass to obtain real time feedback on the baseline knowledge of the students and the subsequent learning that was achieved over one lecture by administering a short MCQ pre-test, followed by a post-test. The questions were projected on the screen and students responded to each question on their own devices. The class results were immediately collated and a comparison of the collective results before and following the lecture was presented graphically as a bar chart. This enabled teachers to see at a glance how many of the class got wrong answers and thus identify where there were general misconceptions. This then made it possible to address these immediately with the whole class. In other words, feedback obtained and given was timely and based on first-hand observation by the teacher, which was consistent with the fundamental principles which underpin good feedback (Krackov, 2009).

Feedback in small group PBL tutorials

In the first few years of medical school at HKU, PBL occupies about 30–40 per cent of the curriculum time. It is conducted in small groups of about ten students, together with a faculty-trained tutor. The students are responsible for working through a clinical case and discussing the issues that arise as information is progressively disclosed. A case is usually revealed over two or three sessions and requires that students search for the information to help them answer the learning objectives they have set for themselves, based on questions which arise during their discussion. Each series of up to five cases is linked to the concurrent teaching (lectures, practicals, skills sessions etc.) taking place in the particular block. One tutor is assigned to the group for the entire series of cases, which takes up to three months to complete. The role of the tutor is to facilitate the discussion and to coach the students through the process of PBL. Tutors are specifically required not to take the role of a lecturer or disseminator of knowledge. More often than not, the tutors are academic staff who are not content experts in the cases being studied.

Example: feedback to students on their performance from tutor and from peers

PBL aims to develop competencies beyond core knowledge. These include 'the development of clinical reasoning, self-directed learning, communication, internal motivation, critical thinking and the ability to work effectively as a team' (Nendaz & Tekian, 1999). The assessment of student performance in PBL is based on five domains (participation, communication, preparation, critical thinking, and group skills) which are graded on a five-point Likert scale according to a set rubric (Figure 2.2). Students are familiar with the expectations and assessment criteria for PBL tutorial sessions and the tutor is responsible for completing this assessment and for discussing it with each student individually at the end of the series.

At the end of each two-hour session, five to ten minutes are reserved for a group review of the PBL process. Students and the tutor step out of their PBL roles and provide, in turn, a candid opinion about how the particular session went. Points raised in the past have included uncertainty about the depth of knowledge required, students who dominate the discussion, and time management. Students work together with the tutor to come to a consensus on how to resolve these issues.

Further formative feedback is provided to students at the halfway point of the tutorial series. Most tutors discuss performance including strengths and areas for improvement with each student individually. Some tutors conduct an open three-way review in which the student, a peer, and the tutor all provide feedback to the student within the group setting, based on the PBL assessment domains. This allows all students to reflect not only on their own performance, but to participate and to practice their appraisal and constructive feedback provision skills.

THE UNIVERSITY OF HONG KONG
LI KA SHING FACULTY OF MEDICINE

M.112/805

Assessment of Individual Student's Performance at PBL Tutorials

Name of student: _____   Group No:_____

Tutor: _____   System / Block: Introduction to the Art and Science of Medicine Block

(Please write all tutors' names if assessed by more than one tutor)

Section I

Please circle your rating of the student in each of the following 5 categories:

A. Participation

Poor	Unsatisfactory	Average	Above Average	Excellent
Little evidence of participation or interest.	Occasionally participates but usually at a superficial level. Shows limited interest.	Makes some contributions, and sometimes suggests learning goals. Shows some interest.	Good participation, and usually shows a deep understanding of the topic. Often suggests hypotheses and learning goals.	Frequent and constructive participation. Always shows a deep understanding. Interested and enthusiastic.

1	2	3	4	5	6	7	8	9	10

Observation / Comment:

B. Communication

Poor	Unsatisfactory	Average	Above Average	Excellent
Poor communication skills. Is unable to express simple ideas	Limited skills. Can express simple concrete ideas	Appropriate communication skills, but has some difficulty with abstract concepts. Tends to read directly from text.	Good skills. Can express complicated ideas using simple language.	Excellent skills. Always able to explain points and views clearly and precisely

1	2	3	4	5	6	7	8	9	10

Observation / Comment:

C. Preparation

Poor	Unsatisfactory	Average	Above Average	Excellent
Little evidence of preparation for tutorials	Some preparation, but usually limited to single source, e.g. textbook or lecture notes.	Sometimes prepares well and uses more than one source, but synthesis sometimes uneven	Usually well prepared. Uses different sources and shows ability to synthesize different perspectives.	Always well prepared, with deep understanding of material from multiple and locally relevant sources.

1	2	3	4	5	6	7	8	9	10

Observation / Comment:

D. Critical Thinking

Poor	Unsatisfactory	Average	Above Average	Excellent
Does not question or challenge others. Does not recognize any errors nor raise any controversies.	Occasionally questions or challenges others. Shows a limited recognition of errors or controversial issues.	Sometimes willing both to challenge others, and to respond to challenges.	Often raises questions that display reflective thinking. Often points out problems or controversies during discussion and pursues further understanding	Can always discuss controversies with reasoning and data. Frequently asks questions that help promote a deeper understanding of the subject.

1	2	3	4	5	6	7	8	9	10

Observation / Comment:

E. Group Skills

Poor	Unsatisfactory	Average	Above Average	Excellent
No apparent idea of group process. Uninvolved.	Passive, with limited group skills. Defensive and resistant when promoted.	Adequate skills. Sometimes a passive member, but responds to prompting.	Good group skills, and contributes actively to group activities. Sometimes helps others.	Excellent group skills. Always attentive and encourages participation by others, but does not dominate the discussion.

1	2	3	4	5	6	7	8	9	10

Observation / Comment:

Section II

Please give your overall comments on the student in the space provided bellow. If you have given any rating below 6 or above 9 in any of the 5 categories, please elaborate on your assessment.

Note: For cases of absence without any reason or justification, a progressive mark deduction system on the assessment will be imposed, e.g. 10% of the overall marks will be deducted for absence from one tutorial, 20% mark deduction for absence from two sessions and so on and no mark will be given in case of absence from more than 50% of the tutorials. Upon receipt of this completed assessment form, the Faculty Office will, taking into account of the attendance record, finalize the marks for each individual student.

SIGNED by: _____   (Tutor)   Date: _____

Figure 2.2   PBL Assessment Template

In fact, these skills appear to be so essential to doctors in training that it has been suggested that the ability to peer evaluate should be considered a core competency, which should be nurtured from an early stage in medical school (Chen, 2012).

The groups in which the authors have tried this approach have been highly receptive to it and quite willing to share their views. Students are informed a week before the midway feedback session that they will be asked to self-evaluate and to provide feedback to one designated peer, chosen at random. Specifically, they are informed that they will need to comment on one perceived strength of their peer, as well as one area for improvement, which reduces the pressure on them to make a 'negative' comment. Interestingly, informal review of this process shows that self- and peer-feedback comments generally align with the views of the tutor. This approach also allows students to take ownership of the evaluation process, and public acknowledgement of the areas in need of improvement provides a clear focus for their efforts over the remaining sessions. By the end of the series of tutorials, students have inevitably made progress in the areas brought to their attention earlier on.

Example: feedback from students to tutor

With the learning process being such a key aspect of successful PBL, all members of the group, including the tutor, must adhere to their roles. At the end of the tutorial series, the tutor receives feedback from the students on his/her effectiveness in:

a. Allowing the group to control the learning process

b. Helping the group focus on the topic

c. Encouraging full participation of all members

d. Providing background information only when necessary

e. Intervening only when appropriate

f. Being attentive to the individual needs of each group member

g. Giving mainly positive feedback to the group

h. Helping the group to think critically and apply new information to the case.

Before this final review, tutors may also engage in self-reflection and invite comments from the group about their effectiveness as part of the

PBL process review at the end of each session. The one-minute-feedback method is another informal means that is used regularly in the program (Angelo & Cross, 1993). Students are asked to write down their responses to one or more short questions which can be tailored to what the teacher would like to elicit feedback on (e.g. How did the teacher help you learn today? What did not work so well for you during this teaching session? What was the muddiest point of the lecture?). In the PBL setting, students are generally asked to list: a) one thing that they have learnt from the current tutorial, and; b) one thing that they would like to be done differently in the next tutorial. These questions are answered anonymously and reviewed by the teacher prior to the following session. At the following session, the teacher makes a point to respond to one or more aspects of the feedback and makes changes as appropriate. The one-minute feedback approach has been shown to be of benefit to both teachers and students, but care must be taken to use the technique selectively as students gradually tire of it, as demonstrated by declining response rates over time (Stead, 2005).

Feedback in clinical teaching environments

Most of the teaching in the latter years of medical school is done in the clinical setting, both in hospital and in the community. Clinical teachers rarely have extended contact with the same students, and therefore students need a consistent means of receiving feedback. Conversely, teachers also need a form of feedback that gives them specific information about their teaching, which they can then act upon. Two examples demonstrating how these issues have been addressed in the family medicine teaching faculty are offered for consideration.

Example: recorded consultation review as feedback to students

One of the learning activities in the final-year family medicine specialty clerkship is a video-recorded consultation review. Students conduct an independent eight-minute clinical consultation with a patient, which is video-recorded. They record information on a standardised form and respond to guiding questions. Each student presents their clinical case to the clinician and a small group of classmates, who view the recording together. Teaching points are elicited for discussion, and observations and comments from the student and peers are encouraged. It has been noted that students are often their own harshest critics.

Video can have many advantages, notably (Moorhead, Maguire, & Thoo, 2004): (a) learners who observe themselves can see their own strengths and weaknesses more readily than if they rely on reflection alone; (b) recordings promote a learner-centred approach with the learner being more actively involved in the analysis; (c) the record prevents disagreement about what actually happened in the consultation; (d) rewinding to a specific point in the consultation can help gain a deeper understanding of what transpired; (e) recordings help feedback to focus on description rather than evaluation – an essential aspect of constructive feedback – and allow issues to be reviewed on several occasions; and (f) recordings allow for feedback from multiple evaluators, which improves reliability, objectivity, and credibility of feedback.

Certain key aspects of the consultation are targeted at assessment via a standardised feedback form, which is completed by the teacher and returned to the student immediately after the session for review. This serves as interim feedback to the student in preparation for the end-of-rotation clinical competency test in which the same criteria are assessed using the identical form. Thus, expectations are made clear, weaknesses are identified, and students are able to practice skills which need improvement during subsequent consultation sessions, prior to the final exam.

Example: student reflective writing as feedback to community-based clinical teachers

During the family medicine junior clerkship, every student works with two different family doctors in the community for two sessions. These attachments provide an opportunity for experiential learning in a real-life setting in which students are given opportunities to perform a clinical consultation with a patient, problem solve the presented symptoms, and gain insight into the work and professional attributes of family doctors in primary care. At the end of the clerkship, one of the required assessment activities is the submission of a logbook, which includes a reflection on the most significant learning experience they had during the clerkship. This provides a unique opportunity to obtain feedback on what students are actually learning from family doctors during the clerkship, and to evaluate whether what they are learning is in fact what they were meant to learn about.

Students suggested that their observation of the doctor-patient relationship left a lasting impression and that they were very aware of the roles of the doctor as a skilled practitioner, a humanist, and an educator, all key elements of professionalism (Chen, 2011). A formal qualitative analysis of the logbook entries submitted in 2011 revealed that the majority of significant learning incidents had an impact on students in four main ways: (1) changing their perception of family medicine; (2) recognising family doctors as positive role models; (3) expanding their view of medicine as a profession; and (4) raising awareness of their own clinical competence (Chen & Chin, 2012). This feedback received from students provides powerful reinforcement to the more than 100 family doctors who take HKU students into their practices on a volunteer basis, illustrating that what students are being taught through role modelling and explicit instruction is being received. It also provides evidence of program goals being met and guiding the direction of further curriculum development or inspiring new complementary initiatives.

Feedback through course evaluation

Student Evaluation of Teaching and Learning (SETL) survey

Introduced in 2009, the Student Evaluation of Teaching and Learning (SETL) survey is one of the ways through which student feedback is collected on courses and instruction at HKU. There have been many studies examining the relationship between student evaluations and student learning. It would be reasonable to assume that if good instruction enhances the learning that takes place, then student evaluations and student learning should be correlated. Reviews of the literature, however, remain inconclusive on this. Attempts to validate the correlation have been complicated by questions of practice, methodology, and interpretation. A meta-analysis of the literature found that a relatively minor relationship exists between learning and the evaluations but that the association is situational and not applicable to all teachers, academic disciplines, or levels of instruction (Clayson, 2009). The primary role of the student feedback obtained through the SETL survey in undergraduate medical education is in course and teacher evaluation, monitoring, and quality assurance. It helps to flag underperforming teachers or courses which may then need closer examination using other mechanisms.

The SETL survey is a two-part questionnaire containing a number of items related to course and teacher effectiveness. There are 21 generic 'core' items in the questionnaire which are used uniformly across all undergraduate courses university-wide (Figure 2.3). In addition to these core items, faculties and programs can apply to add faculty-specific items. All items in the SETL undergo a vetting procedure and require approval by the university's senate. The core items were originally developed, piloted, and validated by the university's Teaching and Learning Quality Committee.

Students are invited to complete the SETL survey towards the end of every undergraduate course. For some courses, this is done in a paper-based format, in others it is done online. To enhance response rates, students are provided class time towards the end of each course to complete the SETL, although they are permitted to complete the survey any time before a set deadline.

The university's Social Sciences Research Centre (SSRC) is tasked with the distribution and processing of the surveys, including preparing SETL reports for courses as well as for individual teachers. In 2012, an online platform was launched allowing students to complete the survey using their own mobile devices. A pilot study conducted to evaluate the effectiveness of the online SETL found that the online administration of the SETL yielded lower response rates than the paper-based format. However, students were much more willing to provide extensive open-ended responses, which program co-ordinators considered to be very valuable for enhancement of teaching and learning. Although many students preferred completing the survey online, there were some concerns regarding anonymity (Social Sciences Research Centre, The University of Hong Kong, 2012). Reports on the questionnaires are generated by the SSRC and provided to the relevant departments as well as to individual teachers for the purpose of identifying issues and enhancing teaching and learning.

The SETL findings are used by course co-ordinators and faculties to identify issues related to course and teacher effectiveness, and it is the responsibility of each program's quality assurance committee to ensure that the findings are monitored and action plans formulated to

	Strongly Disagree	Disagree	Neutral	Agree	Strongly agree
Part I (A) Overall assessment of course effectiveness					
1	I was clear about what I was expected to learn and achieve in this course					
2	The course was well organised in a way that helped me achieve the learning objectives and outcomes					
3	I was able to cope with the course workload					
4	The assessment methods were appropriate in relation to the learning objectives and outcomes of this course					
5	The assessment standards were made clear to me					
6	I feel that I have achieved the learning objectives and outcomes of this course					
7	The course inspired me to pursue further learning in the subject					
8	All things considered, the course was effective in helping me achieve the learning objectives and outcomes					
Part I (B) English as the medium of instruction					
9	English was the medium of instruction in lectures throughout this course					
10	English was the medium of instruction in tutorials throughout this course					
Part I (C) Open–ended comments about the course Write in the space below your comments about this course					
11	What were the best thing(s) about this course?					
12	What thing(s) about this course could be improved?					

	Strongly Disagree	Disagree	Neutral	Agree	Strongly agree
Part II (A) Overall evaluation of teaching					
13	The teacher's explanations helped me achieve the learning objectives and outcomes of this course					
14	I was able to understand the teacher's explanations					
15	The teacher was approachable if I needed help in this course					
16	The teacher provided me with timely and effective feedback					
17	The teacher incorporated elements of interactive teaching					
18	The teacher encouraged interaction and collaboration among students in learning					
19	All things considered, the teacher was effective in helping me achieve the learning objectives and outcomes					
Part II (B) Open–ended comments about the course Write in the space below your comments about this course					
20	What were the best thing(s) about this teacher's teaching?					
21	What thing(s) about this teacher's teaching could be improved?					

Accessed at *http://tl.hku.hk/system/files/Revised_SETL_AppendixA.pdf*

Figure 2.3   Student Evaluation of Teaching and Learning (SETL) core items

address any curricular or program issues for the purpose of enhancing teaching and learning (Figures 2.5 and 2.6). Each year, all faculties are required to submit a *Report on Evaluation of Undergraduate Curricula* to the University which collates information on SETL survey response rates, on problems with administration of the SETL survey, on what teaching and learning issues were identified, and how these issues were dealt with. Course co-ordinators are required to indicate how the SETL results were reviewed, disseminated, and discussed with staff and students.

Using the SETL data, each teacher receives individual teaching evaluation reports on his/her teaching in a particular course. An average score for all teachers involved in the teaching of that course is included as a point of reference. The SETL teaching results are automatically included as one component of the Performance Review and Development (PRD) for professoriate and academic staff, and are used to help identify excellence in teaching as well as teachers who may require support. Other methods such as peer evaluation of teaching are used to supplement student feedback for assessment of teachers.

HKU Student Learning Experience Questionnaire (HKUSLEQ)

HKU conducts institution-wide surveys on students' learning experiences on a regular basis to obtain information for analysis and renewal of curriculum and pedagogy. These are used to help ensure the quality of the students' learning experiences. Each year, all first- and final-year students are invited to complete the *HKU Student Learning Experience Questionnaire* (HKUSLEQ). The questionnaire is shown in Figure 2.4. The survey findings are analyzed and sent back to individual faculties and programs. Discussions are held with deans, associate deans, program directors, and relevant staff members to address issues arising from the findings for the purpose of curriculum and pedagogy monitoring and enhancement. In so doing, students are actively involved and play an integral part in helping to jointly construct the curriculum and the learning (Centre for Teaching and Learning, University of Hong Kong, 2012).

The Institutional Survey Reporting System was launched in 2011 to serve as an online platform for faculties, program co-ordinators, and teachers to retrieve survey results from the HKUSLEQ. The system enables faculties to retrieve survey results and generate reports at

STUDENT PERCEPTIONS ABOUT THEIR LEARNING EXPERIENCES AT HKU

SD = Strongly Disagree; D = Disagree; N = Neutral; A = Agree; SA = Strongly Agree

As a result of my university experience:

	SD	D	N	A	SA
Pursuit of academic / professional excellence					
1. I have developed in depth knowledge in my areas of study.	O	O	O	O	O
2. I strive for excellence in my academic / professional studies.	O	O	O	O	O
Critical intellectual inquiry					
3. My analytical skills have been sharpened.	O	O	O	O	O
4. I am able to look at things from different perspectives.	O	O	O	O	O
Lifelong learning					
5. My enthusiasm for further learning has been stimulated.	O	O	O	O	O
6. I have developed skills which will enable me to engage in life-long learning	O	O	O	O	O
Tackling novel situations and ill-defined problems					
7. I feel confident about tackling unfamiliar problems.	O	O	O	O	O
8. I have learnt how to identify a problem and tackle it.	O	O	O	O	O
9. I feel confident when I am put in a new situation.	O	O	O	O	O
Critical self reflection					
10. I am able to evaluate my academic strengths and weaknesses realistically.	O	O	O	O	O
11. I have become more aware of my personal strengths and weaknesses.	O	O	O	O	O
Greater understanding of others					
12. I am more aware of the thoughts and feelings of other people.	O	O	O	O	O
13. I am more able to see things from other people's points of view.	O	O	O	O	O
Upholding personal and professional ethics					
14. I maintain high standards of personal integrity.	O	O	O	O	O
15. I have learnt to pursue ethical practices in social, academic, and professional settings.	O	O	O	O	O
Intercultural understanding					
16. I am more able to understand similarities and differences between cultures.	O	O	O	O	O
17. I have developed some understanding of people of different cultural and ethnic backgrounds.	O	O	O	O	O
Global citizenship					
18. I am aware of my role as a responsible global citizen.	O	O	O	O	O
19. I am more able to see things from a global perspective.	O	O	O	O	O
Communication					
20. My skills in social communication have been improved.	O	O	O	O	O
21. I am able to communicate my ideas professionally with people	O	O	O	O	O
Collaboration					
22. I have learnt how to collaborate with other people on completing tasks.	O	O	O	O	O
23. I have learnt how to negotiate with others in coming to a decision.	O	O	O	O	O
Leadership					
24. I have acquired leadership skills.	O	O	O	O	O
25. I am confident in taking up a leadership role.	O	O	O	O	O
Advocacy for the improvement of the human condition					
26. My commitment to making the world a better place for all to live in has been enhanced.	O	O	O	O	O
27. I am more aware of issues like human equality, fairness, and justice.	O	O	O	O	O

Perceptions about your program experiences at HKU

Note: The term "teacher(s)" refers to all professors and teaching assistants who have taught you.

SD = Strongly Disagree; D = Disagree; N = Neutral; A = Agree; SA = Strongly Agree

	SD	D	N	A	SA
Active learning					
1. My teachers used a variety of teaching and learning activities	O	O	O	O	O
2. I was given the chance to participate in a variety of activities in class.	O	O	O	O	O
3. My teachers provide opportunities for interaction in class.	O	O	O	O	O
Feedback from teacher					
4. The teachers normally give me helpful feedback on my progress.	O	O	O	O	O
5. The teachers make a real effort to understand difficulties I may be having with my work.	O	O	O	O	O
6. The teachers put a lot of time into commenting on my work.	O	O	O	O	O
Motivation					
7. The teachers of the degree curriculum motivate me to do my best work.	O	O	O	O	O
8. My teachers are extremely good at explaining things.	O	O	O	O	O
9. The teachers work hard to make their subjects interesting.	O	O	O	O	O
Clear goals & standards					
10. I usually have a clear idea of where I am going and what is expected of me in this degree curriculum.	O	O	O	O	O
11. It is always easy to know the standard of work expected.	O	O	O	O	O
12. The teachers made it clear right from the start what they expected from students.	O	O	O	O	O
13. It has often been hard to discover what is expected of me in this degree curriculum.	O	O	O	O	O

	SD	D	N	A	SA
Learning communities					
14. I feel that I am a part of a group of students and teachers who are committed to learning.	O	O	O	O	O
15. I feel I belong to the university community.	O	O	O	O	O
16. I am able to discuss topics of broader intellectual interests with teachers and students.	O	O	O	O	O
Appropriate assessment					
17. I am assessed on how well I can apply what I have learnt to new situations.	O	O	O	O	O
18. I am assessed on my analytical skills.	O	O	O	O	O
19. My teachers ask questions on how well I can integrate knowledge and skills acquired in a course.	O	O	O	O	O
Use of English					
20. I have no difficulties writing assignments in English.	O	O	O	O	O
21. I have no difficulties making oral presentations in English.	O	O	O	O	O
22. I have no difficulties participating in discussion in English.	O	O	O	O	O
23. I have no difficulties reading reference materials in English.	O	O	O	O	O
24. I have no difficulties listening to lectures in English.	O	O	O	O	O
Overall satisfaction					
25. Overall, I am satisfied with the quality of this degree curriculum.	O	O	O	O	O
26. Overall, I am satisfied with the quality of other learning experiences.	O	O	O	O	O

ENGLISH LANGUAGE SUPPORT

(NA = Not Applicable; SD = Strongly Disagree; D = Disagree; N = Neutral; A = Agree; SA = Strongly Agree)

Please indicate to what extent you agree or disagree that the English language support you have received from the following was useful.

	NA	SD	D	N	A	SA
1. Teachers in the Centre for Applied English Studies	O	O	O	O	O	O
2. Teachers in your Department / Faculty	O	O	O	O	O	O

OVERALL COMMENTS

1. The best aspect of my university experience(s) is / are:

2. My university experience could be improved if the university had done the following:

Please provide your Email Address for the Lucky Draw

THANK YOU FOR COMPLETING THIS SURVEY

Accessed at http://tl.hku.hk/wp-content/resources/docs/HKUSLEQSample.pdf

Figure 2.4 HKU Student Learning Experience Questionnaire (HKUSLEQ)

curriculum and program levels, as well as downloading scores for the scales and individual items.

Other forms of collecting student feedback are also used at HKU including:

Staff-Student Consultation Meetings (SSCM)

Small group meetings organized both at the faculty and departmental level and held normally either in the middle of, or by the end of, each block and clerkship rotation. Through these meetings, course, system, and block co-ordinators are able to collect feedback from class and group student representatives. Comments and actions taken are recorded in the meeting notes for attention of the staff and students concerned.

Focus group interviews

On an ad hoc basis when the need arises, the faculty, department or program co-ordinators may seek to hold focus group interviews in selected groups of students to help inform curriculum development and enhancement of teaching and learning. These may result from SETL or HKUSLEQ findings which require further qualitative information to help provide better understanding of unexpected results, or may be more exploratory in nature.

Faculty-co-ordinated paper questionnaires

For stand-alone programmes within the MBBS curriculum, such as the Clinical Visits Program, Patient Care Projects, Special Study Modules, Chinese Medicine Teaching, or Clinical Interpersonal Skills Sessions, which run longitudinally across multiple blocks or clerkships, the faculty initiates 'in-house' student evaluations to collect feedback on the course and teaching. These programs are not covered by the SETL, and the feedback is returned to the program co-ordinator.

Mechanisms for reviewing student evaluations for enhancement of teaching and learning

Collecting student feedback has no value unless it is fully utilized to help enhance teaching and learning. A mechanism needs to be in place to ensure that student feedback is adequately reviewed, action plans devised, properly executed, and followed up. The outcomes of changes need to be monitored to ensure that these changes are effective in enhancing teaching and learning. Smaller course or program or minor intervention changes can be put in place efficiently through planning and co-ordinating committees (Figure 2.5).

Larger clerkship or significant block changes may require vetting and consultation with the MBBS curriculum committee or the faculty board, especially in the case of changes which may affect several departments or programs (Figure 2.6).

To oversee this, the faculty has two monitoring bodies to ensure adequate quality assurance and ongoing quality enhancement: the Faculty Teaching and Learning Quality Committee (FTLQC) and the

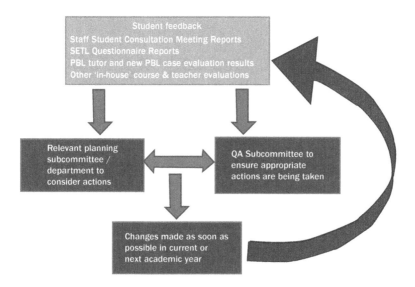

Figure 2.5 Feedback cycle for minor refinements

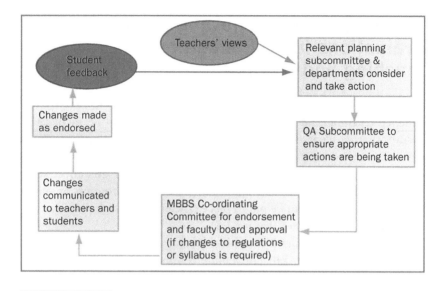

Figure 2.6 Feedback cycle for block or clerkship changes

Quality Assurance Sub-committee of the MBBS Curriculum Committee. Their functions are described below.

Faculty Teaching and Learning Quality Committee (FTLQC)

The aim of the FTLQC is to promote high quality teaching and learning in the faculty. The committee is responsible for ensuring that appropriate quality assurance processes and mechanisms are in place for monitoring, evaluating, and enhancing teaching and learning quality. The FTLQC also co-ordinates the preparation of the annual Student Evaluation of Teaching and Learning (SETL) report for submission to the Senate Teaching and Learning Quality Committee. They are responsible for ensuring that the students' feedback and comments are duly addressed, and they work to promote good practices in teaching and learning and to support pedagogical innovations, in collaboration with the Institute of Medical and Health Sciences Education (IMHSE) of the Faculty.

Quality Assurance Sub-committee of the MBBS Curriculum Committee

The role of the Quality Assurance (QA) Sub-committee is to analyze the feedback and evaluation results collected through various channels, including student surveys, staff-student consultation meetings, and evaluation forms in logbooks. In consultation with the year-specific co-ordinating and planning subcommittees, the QA Sub-committee reports the feedback and evaluation results to departments or individual teachers and advises them on solutions to problems identified in committee reports. The QA Sub-committee is responsible for ensuring that remedial actions are implemented, and for providing regular feedback to students on the remedial actions taken. To facilitate this, protected time is earmarked on student timetables for the purpose of obtaining student feedback each rotation and to provide an opportunity for students to discuss issues with representatives from each relevant teaching department. The faculty ensures that each department provides a formal written response to each issue raised. Individual teachers who require support are encouraged to seek the support of colleagues at the Institute of Medical and Health Sciences Education (IMHSE) to assist with staff development. This may range from assistance in lecture preparation or presentation skills to the option of arranging a formal peer review of teaching.

Evaluation of teaching is a time-consuming and ongoing process, which utilizes many resources. Nonetheless, whether it is an individual evaluating his or her own teaching effectiveness, or a course co-ordinator using the information to re-design a whole program, student feedback is an essential component of both professional development and curriculum monitoring and assurance. Having a wide variety of types of information obtained from multiple sources will help to ensure that the feedback obtained is as comprehensive as possible. Having mechanisms in place to ensure that feedback and evaluation findings are dealt with in a timely and appropriate manner will help teachers know that they are achieving their teaching goals, and facilitate a better learning environment for students.

Conclusion

Student feedback is an essential aspect of curriculum development, which must be built into any program from the outset. This chapter has provided a snapshot of how student feedback is received by teachers in order to allow them to improve their teaching and how it is given in a timely fashion to allow individual students to act and improve before they are assessed. The approaches described are not universally practiced within the Faculty of Medicine at HKU, and there may be other effective techniques adopted by individual teachers. As such, it is suggested in this chapter that continuing staff development and sharing in the area of student feedback in order to systematize and disseminate best practice is an area for further action. It is also suggested here that systemic collection of generic feedback for institutional use (e.g. to facilitate comparison between faculties), combined with more specific feedback relating to particular programs (e.g. to acquire detailed information about unique features of a program) are both important in providing an overview of how well courses, programs, departments, or faculties are performing against their intended aims and where improvements need to be made.

References

The 6-Year Medical Curriculum Handbook. (2012). *Li Ka Shing Faculty of Medicine University of Hong Kong.*

Angelo, T. A., & Cross, P. K. (1993). *Classroom Assessment Techniques.* San Francisco: Jossey-Bass.

Brown, G., & Manogue, M. (2001). AMEE Medical Education Guide No. 22: Refreshing lecturing: a guide for lecturers. *Medical Teacher, 23*(3), 231–244.

Cain, J., Black, E. P., & Rohr, J. (2009). An audience response system strategy to improve student motivation, attention and feedback. *American Journal of Pharmaceutical Edcucation, 73*(2), 21.

Centre for Teaching and Learning, The University of Hong Kong. (2012). Evaluation of Teaching and Learning. *http://tl.hku.hk/tl/evaluation/.*

Chen, J. (2012). Why peer evaluation by students should be part of the medical school learning environment. *Medical Teacher, 34*(8), 603–606.

Chen, J. Y. (2011). What students are really learning from family doctors: professionalism in practice. *Hong Kong Practitioner, 33*, 137–138.

Chen, J. Y., & Chin, W. Y. (2012). *Critical learning incidents in a year 3 family medicine clerkship.* Paper presented at the Hong Kong Primary Care Conference, Hong Kong.

Clayson, D. E. (2009). Student evaluations of teaching: are they related to what students learn?: A Meta-Analysis and Review of the Literature. *Journal of Marketing Education, 31*(1), 16–30.

Dent, J. A., & Harden, R. M. (Eds.). (2009). *A Practical Guide for Medical Teachers* (Third ed.). Edinburgh: Churchill Livingtone Elsevier.

Dornan, T., Mann, K., Scherpbier, A., & Spencer, J. (Eds.). (2011). *Medical Education Theory and Practice*. Edinburgh: Churchill Livingstone Elsevier.

Fok, W. (2012). HKU iClass offical website, from *http://www.eee.hku.hk/~iclass/*

Krackov, S. K. (2009). Giving feedback. In J. Dent & R. Harden (Eds.), *A Practical Guide for Medical Teachers* (Third ed., pp. 357–367). Edinburgh: Churchill Livingstone Elsevier.

Moorhead, R., Maguire, P., & Thoo, S., Lee. (2004). Giving feedback to learners in the practice. *Australian family physician, 33*(9), 691–695.

Nair, C. S., & Mertova, P. (Eds.). (2011). *Student Feedback*. Oxford: Chandos Publishing.

Nendaz, M. R., & Tekian, A. (1999). Assessment in problem-based learning medical schools: a literature review. *Teaching and Learning in Medicine, 11*(4), 232–243.

Social Sciences Research Centre, The University of Hong Kong. (2012). Student evaluation of teaching. *http://www.ssrc.hku.hk/web/setl.html*, (accessed July 2013).

Stead, D. R. (2005). A review of the one-minute paper. *Active Learning in Higher Education, 6*(2), 118–131.

Feedback as Conceptualised and Practised in South East Asia

Gominda Ponnamperuma,
Faculty of Medicine, University of Colombo, Sri Lanka

Abstract: Feedback, though a universal phenomenon that has global acceptance and currency, is both conceptualised and practised variably in different parts of the world. This chapter investigates how feedback is conceptualised, practised, and could be improved, both from medical students' and teachers' perspective, in the socio-cultural milieu of South East Asia.

There are two main types of feedback: feedback to students (i.e. feedback on learning), and feedback by students (i.e. feedback on teaching). Most of the principles of good feedback apply to both types. Hence, feedback to students will be first elaborated upon in this chapter, followed by a case study on feedback by students.

How feedback is conceptualised, both by students and teachers, is addressed by investigating the extent to which feedback is conceived to be: a two-way process; confidential; free of repercussions; reinforcing good behaviour; identifying undesirable behaviour and providing options to alter such behaviour; supportive; enhancing creativity; a challenge to step outside of one's comfort zone, and an opportunity to monitor progress.

How feedback is practised is discussed by considering the extent to which feedback is: timely; clear; based upon agreed goals; built upon first-hand information; addressing behaviour rather than personality traits; specific rather than general; non-judgemental; balanced; selective; practical (i.e. realistic – dealing with what is achievable); constructive; proactive (rather than solely reactionary); actionable (i.e. leads to a pragmatic action plan), and carried out in a conducive environment.

Improving the practice of feedback is outlined by analysing the extent to which some of the well documented unhealthy practices are present in medical schools in the local set-up, and how some of these could best be ameliorated. These unhealthy practices could be related to the feedback provider or the feedback recipient. Those related to the feedback provider are: being obligatory and too prescriptive; projecting a moral high ground; burying and fudging; minimising negative feedback, and clouding. Those related to the feedback recipient are mainly associated with negative feedback; e.g. denial, blaming, rationalisation, and anger.

Hence the success of the entire feedback process is determined by the extent to which the process has been conceptualised (i.e. by identifying what is required) appropriately, and is carried out accordingly to achieve the conceptualised goals, using educationally sound practices, while avoiding unhealthy practices.

Keywords: Teacher feedback; student feedback; medical education; reflection

Introduction

Feedback has many definitions and connotations. In scientific parlance, feedback refers to the reintroduction of information from a prior activity, so that the next or current activity of a process can be modulated, if necessary. The next or the current activity could be a totally new one, or a repetition or an extension of the same one. In teaching and learning, feedback operates in the same way.

An educational process could be learning, teaching, assessment, or any combination of the said three processes. The reintroduction of information from a previous activity back to the current or future educational process could be from an external and/or internal source(s).

If a 'learning' process is considered, external sources are teachers, peers, examination results and examiners, and the internal source is the learners themselves. However, if a 'teaching' process is considered, external sources are students, peers, quality assurance reports, examination results and examiners, while 'internal source' refers to the teachers themselves. Similarly from an 'assessment' point of view, the external sources indicate candidates, external examiners and quality assurance reports, and the internal sources are the examiners organising the examination, and the examination results. In this chapter, feedback is primarily considered in the light of a learning process. However, to illustrate the key principles of feedback related to a teaching process, a case study relating to the latter is discussed towards the end of the chapter.

Any activity will have a process and a product. Feedback can relate to either or both. Depending on the level of competence of the performer, feedback on the process can also be subdivided into feedback on the immediate process (i.e. the individual steps) and on the overall process (i.e. how the individual steps are combined into an integrated act). This chapter addresses feedback related to both the process and the product.

Finally, feedback can be either explicit or implicit. Implicit feedback is vague and confusing. Hence, only explicit feedback delivered using oral and written media will be considered in this chapter.

Following is an exploration of feedback as practised in South East Asia, focussing primarily on the learning and teaching process; from the point of view of both the feedback provider and receiver; based on both the process and the product of feedback; collected using both internal and external sources; and offered explicitly in the form of both oral and written media. Since literature is sparse on feedback as practised in the South East Asian region, this chapter should be viewed as an exposition of the basic tenets of feedback as practised within the region, based on both the literature, where available, and the author's own experience.

Feedback on the learning process

The following discussion on feedback to students (i.e. on the learning process) is categorised into conceptualisation of feedback, practice of feedback, and improving feedback.

How feedback is conceptualised

A two-way process

Feedback, delivered in person to an individual or to a group, has to be considered as a two-way process (Krackov, 2009) that encourages not only active provision, but also active reception. The recipient, actively taking part in the feedback process, may clarify unclear elements in it (Rudland et al, 2013), confirm the understanding by reframing or rephrasing the feedback, and request specific examples of some of the elements in the feedback. Hence, both the provider and the recipient should be on the same wavelength. This implies a non-hierarchical setting where the provider and the recipient, while respecting their clearly defined roles, can challenge one another constructively.

It would be fair to conclude that, though there may be exceptions, by and large, such open dialogue on equal terms is not entirely prevalent in the local setting, especially related to clinical training, when giving and receiving feedback. This could be due primarily to the hierarchical nature of the environs, where the role of the feedback provider is assumed to be solely to deliver the feedback, with the recipient's role being confined to passively receiving feedback.

Confidentiality

Feedback, when positive, can be public; the recipient may like such feedback. When negative, however, feedback should be private and confidential (Clynes & Raftery, 2008), giving due consideration to the emotions of the recipient (Hewson & Little, 1998; Kelly, 2007). If it has to be group feedback, then it should be worded in such a way that the recipients can extract the general learning points, but cannot personally identify those at whom feedback is directed.

Group feedback is not uncommon in the region, due mainly to high student/staff ratios and to group learning processes, such as problem-based learning, learning in clinical groups, and group research projects commonly practised in medical education. In such situations, if the feedback provider is not sufficiently sensitive to the recipients' needs and emotions, negative feedback may lead to a situation where the recipients cease to welcome feedback in general. A systemic feedback phobia may set in. As a consequence, the recipients may develop defensive attitudes to feedback, and also become reticent in exposing themselves to tutors or feedback providers.

Freedom from repercussions

Even in the post-behaviourism era, positive feedback with praise and reward is considered desirable. However, providing negative feedback need not and should not entail any further punishment. Negative feedback itself should be a strong enough repercussion. Moreover, there should not be any punitive consequences to feedback, especially negative feedback. The only consequences should be simple and agreed upon monitoring strategies, arising directly from feedback.

Within the region, feedback has not been entirely well-conceptualised, both by the feedback provider and recipient. As a result, there have been instances where negative feedback has led to further repercussions, such as non-signing off of clinical rotations. These repercussions have mostly not been related to pre-agreed consequences understood by both the feedback provider and the receiver. Hence, there is a perceived mismatch between the expectations of the provider and receiver (Liberman et al, 2005; Perera et al, 2008).

Reinforcing good behaviour

To reinforce good behaviour (Thorndike, 1931) simple actions such as 'praising' (Wilkinson, 1981) are a tool that can be used judiciously. Notwithstanding the reservations expressed by Deci et al (1999), if the opportunity warrants, the provider can also resort to rewarding desirable behaviour more substantially.

Within the local setting, reinforcing desirable behaviour is rather conservative, when compared to the western world. For example, in quantitative feedback (e.g. assessment ratings such as in workplace-based assessment and in Objective Structured Clinical Examinations), it is rare that desirable behaviour receives the highest available rating. This results in ratings within a restricted range; e.g. a five-point rating scale being reduced in practice to a four-point rating scale.

Identifying undesirable behaviour and providing options to alter it

Identifying undesirable behaviour, though a key feature in feedback (Cantillon & Sargeant, 2008), requires caution, as it may typify negative feedback. Identifying undesirable behaviour is commonly practised in the region. However, such feedback is not always backed up with options for improvement. Hence, established models of feedback in medical education such as Pendleton's rules (Pendleton et al., 2013) should be encouraged more actively through extensive staff development within the region.

Supporting learners

Feedback, when supportive (Rudland et al, 2013), not only triggers the identification of options to correct undesirable behaviour, but also directs the learner (i.e. feedback recipient) to appropriate resources so that the learner can apply those corrective measures. For example, supportive feedback is not only stating:

> It would be useful for you to brush up your knowledge on ...
> you could do this by referring to your own notes, reading
> a textbook, or using an authoritative website,

but also stating:

> To brush up your knowledge on ... there is a good book called
> 'x' in the library and also there is a good website named 'xx'.

The former is identifying undesirable behaviour and providing options to correct it, while the latter could be more specifically termed as being supportive, especially if the provider believes that the recipient is struggling to identify sound resource material.

Where feedback takes place, supportive feedback may not be entirely uncommon within the region. However, since, in general, feedback does not happen with the frequency that it should happen, supportive feedback is invariably under-utilised.

Enhancing creativity

When providing especially negative feedback (Baron, 1988), with not only options for improvement but also support for improvement, the creativity of both the feedback provider and the recipient may trigger the generation of novel approaches to the provision of feedback and improvement. Such an approach has given rise to a well-known model called the 'sandwich model' of feedback, where negative feedback is both preceded and followed by positive feedback (Dohrenwend, 2002).

Creativity requires time and concerted effort. Such commodities (i.e. time and effort for feedback) are not commonplace within the region, especially among teachers who are busy clinicians manning busy clinics. However, another more pertinent reason may be a lack of a proper theoretical framework to conceptualise the importance and the methods of giving feedback.

Challenging one's comfort zone

Challenging the recipient to achieve greater heights, notwithstanding the fact that the recipient has achieved the targeted learning, can be a profoundly powerful impact of well-directed feedback. It is this characteristic of feedback that is not sufficiently addressed by definitions that conceptualise feedback as information that helps the learner bridge the gap between the present state and desired state; i.e. where they should be (Hattie & Timperley, 2007). Strictly following such definitions implies that if the learner has already reached the desired state, challenging the learner's comfort zone becomes redundant. Even within this definition the desired state should not be fixed, but be dynamic, so that it can be set and re-set as the learner progresses along the journey of learning, depending upon their level of achievement.

Challenging the learner's comfort zone, in the local setting, is a technique mostly utilised with students who are at either end of the ability spectrum; i.e. the best and worst students. It is more likely that these students have a tendency to confine themselves to their comfort zones. The best students do so since they have achieved what is required, and worst students do so due to sheer lack of initiative and motivation.

Opportunities to monitor progress

Feedback, based on frameworks such as Pendleton's rules (Pendleton et al, 2003), should lead to a discussion on what can be improved. The action plan, agreed through such a discussion, needs to be monitored regularly to check whether the desired goal is being achieved. Towards this end, monitoring progress is indispensable.

Due to lack of resources (e.g. time) and lack of proper conceptualisation of feedback, monitoring of progress, most of the time, is practised haphazardly in the local context. Institutionalisation of a proper system of feedback, by the introduction of a process such as workplace-based assessment, which can be used to profile the students and monitor their progress over time, is a possible solution that could overcome this deficiency.

How feedback is carried out

Timeliness

The general rule is that feedback needs to be immediate (Rudland et al, 2010). This is because feedback should be carried out when the memory of the behaviour on which feedback is given is fresh in the minds of both the provider and recipient. More importantly, however, feedback should occur at a time when the recipient is prepared to receive such information. Hence, rather than adhering rigidly to the principle of offering immediate feedback, it is important to determine the timing sensibly (Ende, 1983). For example, in a busy clinical setting, if there is no opportunity or space for detailed feedback that requires reflective exploration of a complex task (Archer, 2010), then it is best to document the event and postpone feedback to the next available opportunity. In the local setting, feedback always tends to be immediate, mainly because it is provided mostly as verbal, and often group, feedback. Hence, there is less opportunity for the timing of feedback to be based upon educational considerations and the needs of the recipient. This may be mostly due to resource constraints, where finding time on another occasion to give feedback may not always be practical due to the busy lifestyle and work schedule of most clinicians. More importantly, however, it may also be due to lack of understanding of the process of feedback and a general reluctance to document the feedback that should be given, so that it could be better given on another occasion.

Based upon agreed goals

Focussed feedback is the most productive. For this, the goals of feedback (Kanfer & Ackerman, 1989) need to be explicitly communicated to and negotiated with the recipient.

In the South East Asia region, however, the goals of feedback tend to be implicit rather than explicit. This is partly because of the general reluctance on the part of the provider to follow the established guidelines of giving feedback, by first arriving at a consensus on the goals of feedback with the recipient.

Clear

Only feedback that can be understood by the recipient exactly in the way that it was meant to be will lead to the intended goals of learning. To this end, it is good practice for the provider to check the understanding of feedback by offering an opportunity to raise questions or to clarify or rephrase any doubts (Clynes & Raftery, 2008).

In the region, feedback, in general, is clear and to-the-point. However, the opportunity to clarify and question the provider is either not always available or, even if such opportunity is available, recipients are rather reluctant to make the best use of such opportunities. This may be partly due to the hierarchical relationship that exists between the clinician teacher and the student.

Other important aspects of high-quality feedback include:

- Building it on firsthand information which could only have been obtained through direct observation of the recipient by the feedback provider (Cantillon & Sargeant, 2008)
- Addressing behaviour rather than personal traits (Narciss & Huth, 2004; Baard & Neville, 1996)
- Addressing specific concerns rather than general ones (Moreno, 2004)
- Being non-judgemental, as passing judgements does not promote reflection (Cantillon & Sargeant, 2008)
- Balance
- Selectiveness
- Practicality (i.e. it is realistic – dealing with what is achievable)
- Constructiveness (Bienstock et al., 2007; Hattie & Timperley, 2007)
- It encourages proactivity
- It is actionable (i.e. it leads to a pragmatic action plan)
- It is carried out in a conducive environment (Clynes & Raftery, 2008).

Hence, specific models of feedback, such as the 'sandwich model' (Dohrenwend, 2002), have been developed to avoid giving only negative feedback. In the region, negative feedback tends to supersede positive feedback, both in the clinical and non-clinical setting. This tendency probably has a cultural explanation.

Improving current practice

Ways of improving current practices can only be ascertained by first reviewing current unhealthy practices. Following is a brief exploration of common unhealthy practices related to providers and recipients.

Unhealthy practices related to the feedback provider

Being obligatory and too prescriptive

Feedback needs to be specific. However, if the feedback provider takes specificity to a level that, rather than offering several specific options to the recipient, insists on a particular option that the recipient must select, then such feedback becomes obligatory and too prescriptive; i.e. too directive as opposed to being facilitative (Archer, 2010). Instead, feedback, while being specific, should be sufficiently flexible to allow the recipient to figure out, perhaps with the guidance of the provider, the best option available.

Prescriptive feedback has been ingrained in the culture of many medical education settings to such an extent that recipients expect the provider to be prescriptive. Although in some specific instances, where there is only one correct way of performing, as in the training of highly technical skills (e.g. endoscopic procedures), such recipient expectations may be legitimate, in most instances the consequence of prescriptive feedback is the production of an over-dependent recipient with poor self-confidence and initiative. To overcome such an outcome, training both the provider and the recipient when to give and expect (respectively) prescriptive feedback appears mandatory.

Projecting a moral high ground

Closely linked with the hierarchical relationship between the provider and recipient is the feedback provider taking high moral ground. There may be advantages in the recipient viewing the provider as a superhuman, know-it-all person; in the eyes of the recipient, this enhances the credibility of feedback (Eraut, 2006). Such assumptions may lead to disillusionment, however, if the recipient later finds out that the provider does have deficiencies. Also, viewing the provider as superhuman can create an artificial gap between the recipient and the provider that inhibits proper rapport building and exchange of ideas.

This again is prevalent in at least some settings in the region, especially in the context of novice trainees learning highly specialised clinical skills. Training both providers and recipients using case discussions to create an awareness of this pitfall would be a sound methodology, as it is only by being consciously vigilant about this unhealthy practice that it can be avoided.

Other unhealthy practices include:

- Burying and fudging, which may result when the provider attempts not to hurt the recipient with negative feedback (Clynes, 2008)
- Minimising negative feedback (which is rare in the South East Asian setting)
- Clouding (i.e. providing conflicting end points).

Unhealthy practices related to the feedback recipient

These are mainly related to negative feedback. Following is an outline of some of the main recipient-related unhealthy practices.

- Denial

This is a natural human response to any negative or unpleasant experience. Hence it is prevalent, especially when negative feedback is provided within groups of recipients. This is mainly due to the perceived fear of a dent in self-esteem (Kluger & DeNisi, 1996).

- Blaming, rationalisation, or anger

Additional defence mechanisms (Krackov, 2009) that recipients may adopt to project a shortcoming on (or attribute a shortcoming to) someone or something else.

Considering the aforementioned, it is clear that training (Henderson et al., 2005) must take centre stage in overcoming all these unhealthy practices, be they related to the provider or the recipient. Training, however, should be focused not only on how to avoid the unhealthy practices, but also on how to make the most of the healthy practices. Adopting a variety of healthy practices in combination (Carr, 2006), may bring about the best results.

Feedback on the teaching process

Following is a case study that highlights how not only feedback to students, but feedback by students, can be used to reform the teaching process.

Context

The curriculum of the Faculty of Medicine, University of Colombo, Sri Lanka, has five major streams: Basic Sciences Stream; Applied Sciences Stream; Clinical Sciences Stream; Community Stream; and Behavioural Sciences Stream (BSS). The Basic Sciences Stream provides students with the knowledge of basic science necessary to study medicine (e.g. anatomy, physiology, and biochemistry). The Applied Sciences Stream, which occupies the major portion of the curriculum, imparts learning that integrates both basic and para-clinical sciences (e.g. pathology, microbiology, pharmacology) with clinical sciences (e.g. internal medicine, obstetrics and gynaecology, surgery, paediatrics), using several body system-based modules (e.g. cardiovascular system module). The Clinical Sciences Stream deals with clinical training, while reinforcing and integrating the essential theoretical knowledge offered through the other streams. Through the Community Stream, students learn about public- and community-health related aspects of medicine (e.g. epidemiology, health promotion, disease prevention), while the Behavioural Sciences Stream updates students on the humanistic aspects of medical practice (e.g. medical ethics, communication skills, professionalism). It is customary for each stream to obtain student feedback both formally and informally. Formal feedback is obtained through surveys and focus group discussions, while informal discussions with students and student representatives by faculty provide informal feedback. In addition, there are formal student surveys conducted periodically to evaluate the implementation of the entire curriculum (i.e. all five streams). This case study describes how the feedback received from students on the teaching and learning of the BSS was acted upon.

The BSS curriculum is organised as several modules (e.g. ethics module, communication skills module). The teaching and learning in the BSS is carried out throughout the curriculum, but more intensely during the first four years, in parallel to the teaching and learning of other streams. Although students are encouraged to apply the theory that they gain on behavioural sciences to practice during all stages of the curriculum, in the fifth and final year the students are expected to apply the learning that they gained in the first four years more holistically and more rigorously to practice. The teaching and learning is achieved in the first four years mainly through lectures followed by small group discussions. The small group discussions provide an opportunity to apply the theory taught in lectures to simulated situations which are mainly paper-based scenarios. At the end of each module, the students are tested on the application of knowledge to simulated, paper-based situations using structured essay questions. This is in addition to an end-of-stream assessment that follows the same format of structured essay questions.

Feedback

Informal discussions as well as formal focus group discussions with students revealed that students could not relate the teaching and learning of the BSS to their future practice of medicine. The majority of students viewed behavioural sciences as a subject that they need to learn to pass the assessment. Below are examples of typical student comments on teaching and learning in the BSS:

> 'Beyond studying to pass the exam, I do not see how behavioural sciences are practised in actual situations.'

> 'We cannot relate behavioural sciences to the medical practice that we see in the hospital.'

> 'I study behavioural sciences in isolation, as a separate subject.'

Acting upon feedback

The above finding, that students considered teaching and learning in the BSS as theoretical, with little or no relevance to practice, was made despite the fact that both learning and assessment within the BSS were heavily focused on application of knowledge to simulated situations. Hence, it was clear that offering behavioural sciences in the form of theory, and a series of simulated, paper-based situations in which to apply theory, had not made the intended impact. Thus, there was a case for offering behavioural sciences in a more practical and holistic way, so that students considered the theoretical content of behavioural sciences as an essential part of sound medical practice, rather than a standalone subject. To remedy this, it was decided to introduce the following three interventions:

(a) To continue with the simulated, paper-based scenarios, as this is the most feasible and realistic, given the resource constraints, but re-design the scenarios, so that these scenarios are related to the medical modules that the students learn in parallel at any given time. For example, if the module on the cardiovascular system is conducted in the Applied Sciences Stream, at a time when the ethics module is studied in the BSS, then the paper-based, simulated scenarios in the BSS for small group discussions will be focussed on patients with ethical issues related to cardiovascular medicine. This alignment of the BSS teaching and learning with other parts of the curriculum is thought to enhance the applicability of the BSS learning to other (more medically-oriented) parts of the curriculum.

(b) To continue with the structured essay type of assessment, as this is most feasible, but look into the possibility of building questions related to behavioural sciences within the structured essay questions of other modules. For example, in the cardiovascular system module, if there is a structured essay question based on a patient needing coronary angioplasty, apart from asking about the anatomy of coronary circulation and the pathology of atherosclerosis, a part of the question could be on taking informed consent for angioplasty.

(c) To explore whether application of behavioural sciences could be assessed within the clinical context, using workplace-based assessment.

While (a) above has already been implemented, (b) and (c) are still being considered for implementation.

All the above measures address the educational principle of 'integrated learning', which in turn forms the basis of student feedback related to less than optimal learning in the BSS. Since the behavioural sciences were learnt in isolation, notwithstanding the fact that the learning constituted the application of behavioural science knowledge to clinically relevant paper-based scenarios, the students failed to appreciate the relevance of behavioural sciences to medical practice.

As well as integrated learning, this case study also highlights some of the key educational principles related to feedback. They are as follows:

- Interventions to address negative feedback should be focussed on the core issue(s) raised by feedback (i.e. in this case study the poor appreciation by students of how behavioural sciences were applied to practice).

- If the issue communicated through feedback is complex, such as that illustrated in this case study, multiple rather than singular, one-off interventions are more likely to succeed.

- Interventions need to be the 'most practical', rather than the 'best'. For example, in the above situation, the 'best' option for increasing the relevance may be to introduce a fully-fledged portfolio assessment system with a battery of workplace-based assessments. However, if the resources do not permit such an intervention, then a scaled down version of the same intervention such as intervention (c) above could be considered.

Hence, this case study illustrates how feedback from students can be used to initiate educationally sound curriculum interventions to facilitate more meaningful student learning. Once these interventions are well established, the feedback loop can be completed by seeking student feedback again to verify whether the intended benefits of the interventions have been accrued.

Conclusion

Feedback, like any activity, has a beginning, a process and an end. The beginning needs a proper preparation. For such preparation, conceptualising feedback as a well-organised, academic activity, in line with the considerations explored in this chapter under 'how feedback is conceptualised' is mandatory. Based on such conceptualisation, feedback on any given occasion should be shaped to enhance its benefit to the recipient, be it the student or the teacher. The practice points discussed in this chapter under the heading 'how feedback is carried out' can be helpful in achieving this end. To improve practice by avoiding some of the well-documented pitfalls, both the recipient and the provider of feedback need to be trained to steer consciously away from the unhealthy practices mentioned under 'improving practice' in the chapter. Such a well thought-out process should result in the heralding of a new beginning by means of an action plan, based on reflective practice.

References

Archer, JC. (2010). State of the science in health professional education: effective feedback. *Medical Education*, 44: 101–108.

Baard P, Neville S. (1996). The intrinsically motivated nurse: help and hindrance from evaluation feedback sessions. *Journal of Nursing Administration*, 26 (7/8): 19–26.

Baron RA. (1988). Negative effects of destructive criticism: impact on conflict, self-efficacy, and task performance. *Journal of Applied Psychology*, 73: 199–207.

Bienstock JL, Katz NT, Cox SM, Hueppchen N, Erickson S, Puscheck EE. (2007). To the point: medical education reviews--providing feedback. *American Journal of Obstetrics and Gynaecology*, 196(6): 508–513.

Cantillon, P, Sargeant J. (2008). Giving feedback in clinical settings. *British Medical Journal*, 337: 1292–1294.

Carr S. (2006). The Foundation Programme assessment tools. An opportunity to enhance feedback to trainees? *Postgraduate Medical Journal*, 82: 576–579.

Clay AS, Que L, Petrusa ER, Sebastian M, Govert J. (2007). Debriefing in the intensive care unit: a feedback tool to facilitate bedside teaching. *Critical Care Medicine*, 35(3): 738–754.

Clynes M. (2008). Providing feedback on clinical performance to student nurses in children's nursing: challenges facing preceptors. *Journal of Children's and Young People's Nursing*, 2(1): 29–35.

Clynes MP, Raftery SEC. (2008). Feedback: An essential element of student learning in clinical practice. *Nurse Education in Practice*, 8: 405–411.

Deci EL, Koestner R, Ryan MR. (1999). A meta-analytic review of experiments examining the effects of extrinsic rewards on intrinsic motivation. *Psychological Bulletin*, 125: 627–668.

Dohrenwend A. (2002). Serving up the feedback sandwich. *Family Practice Management*, 9 (10): 43–49.

Ende, J. (1983). Feedback in clinical medical education. *Journal of the American Medical Association*, 250: 777–781.

Eraut, M. (2006). Feedback. *Learning in Health and Social Care*, 5(3): 111–118.

Hattie J, Timperley H. (2007). The Power of Feedback. *Review of Educational Research*, 77: 81–112.

Henderson P, Ferguson-Smith AC, Johnson MH. (2005). Developing essential professional skills: a framework for teaching and learning about feedback. *BioMedical Central Medical Education*, 5: 1–6. Available at: *http://www.biomedcentral.com/content/pdf/1472-6920-5-11.pdf* (Accessed on 1 August 2013).

Hewson MG, Little ML. (1998). Giving feedback in medical education. *Journal of General Internal Medicine*, 13(2): 111–116.

Kanfer R, Ackerman PL. (1989). Motivation and cognitive abilities: an integrative/aptitude-treatment interaction approach to skill acquisition. *Journal of Applied Psychology*, 74: 657–690.

Kelly C. (2007). Students' perceptions of effective clinical teaching revisited. *Nurse Education Today*, 27: 885–892.

King J. (1999). Giving feedback. *British Medical Journal*, 318(7200): 1–3.

Kluger AN, DeNisi A. (1996). The effects of feedback interventions on performance: A historical review, a meta-analysis, and a preliminary feedback intervention theory. *Psychological Bulletin*, 119(2): 254–284.

Kolb, D.A. (1984) *Experiential Learning: Experience as the source of learning and development.* Englewood Cliffs, Prentice Hall, New Jersey. p. 4.

Krackov SK. (2009). Giving Feedback. Ch. 47 In: Dent J & Harden RM. (eds) *A Practical Guide for Medical Teachers*. Churchill Livingstone Elsevier, UK. p. 357–367.

Liberman AS, Liberman M, Steinert Y, McLeod P, Meterissian S. (2005). Surgery residents and attending surgeons have different perceptions of feedback. *Medical Teacher*, 27(5): 470–472.

Moreno R. (2004). Decreasing cognitive load for novice students: effects of explanatory versus corrective feedback in discovery-based multimedia. *Instructional Science*, 32: 99–113.

Narciss S, Huth K. (2004). How to design informative tutoring feedback for multimedia learning. In: Niegemann HM, Leutner D, Brunken R. (eds.) *Instructional Design for Multimedia Learning.* Waxmann, Munster, New York. p. 181–195.

Pendleton D, Schofield T, Tate P, Havelock P. (2003). *The New Consultation: Developing Doctor-Patient Communication.* Oxford University Press, Oxford. p. 3.

Perera J, Lee N, Win K, Perera J, Wijesuriya L. (2008). Formative feedback to students: the mismatch between faculty perceptions and student expectations. *Medical Teacher,* 30: 395–399.

Rudland J, Bagg W, Child S, de Beer W, Hazell W, Poole P, Sheehan D, Wilkinson TJ. (2010). Maximising learning through effective supervision. *New Zealand Medical Journal,* 123: 117–126.

Rudland J, Wilkinson T, Wearn A, Nicol P, Tunny T, Owen C, O'Keefe M. (2013). A student-centred feedback model for educators. *Clinical Teacher,* 10(2): 99–102.

Sargeant JM, Mann KV, Van der Vleuten CP, Metsemakers JF. (2009). Reflection: a link between receiving and using assessment feedback. *Advances in Health Sciences Education Theory and Practice,* 14(3): 399–410.

Thorndike EL. (1931). *Human Learning.* Century, New York. p. 162–181.

Wilkinson SS. (1981). The relationship of teacher praise and student achievement: A meta-analysis of selected research. *Dissertation Abstracts International,* 41(9-A): 3998.

Enhancing Clinical Education with Student Feedback: a Thai Perspective

Cherdsak Iramaneerat,
Department of Surgery, Faculty of Medicine,
Siriraj Hospital, Mahidol University

Abstract: Feedback is an important part of adult learning. Not only learners, but also teachers, can benefit from receiving feedback. Student feedback provides important perspectives on the quality of instruction and assessment, which a medical faculty should not neglect. This chapter provides a description of how student feedback is obtained and used in one medical faculty in Thailand. The author shows evidence for and against the use of student feedback. The author then describes the medical education system in Thailand. The cultural differences between Thailand and western societies are also discussed. The author then shares the experience of the use of student feedback at the Faculty of Medicine, Siriraj Hospital, Mahidol University. Examples are given to show how feedback has been obtained, and how it has been used to improve the medical curriculum in various aspects, including: individual teachers, teaching strategies, courses, curriculum, and the assessment approaches. The use of feedback is discussed both in the context of undergraduate education and postgraduate training.

Keywords: Student feedback; medical school; Thailand

Introduction

Feedback is information given to learners with the goal of improving those learners' future performance. It is widely accepted that feedback is an integral part of adult learning as well as clinical education

(Coles, 1998; van de Ridder, Stokking, McGaghie, & Cate, 2008). From the perspective of deliberate practice, feedback is an important part of attaining an expert level of performance (Ericsson, 2006; Ericsson, Krampe, & Tesch-Romer, 1993). Educators realise the benefits of feedback in improving student learning. Medical teachers are encouraged to give students feedback to improve their clinical performance (Sargeant & Mann, 2010). Many higher education programs have moved forward in training faculty members to provide effective feedback to their students and residents, and these efforts have yielded significant benefits to students' learning.

However, students should not be the only party to gain benefits from receiving feedback. Medical teachers should also realise that teaching skills are acquired skills that can be improved through the process of deliberate practice. Thus, teachers should be able to improve performance by listening to students' feedback. Student feedback provides important perspectives on teaching quality that medical school faculty should not neglect. Furthermore, many medical teachers also get involved in designing courses or revising curricula. Such a process often involves assessing what kind of knowledge, skills, or attitudes students or residents would need to develop effectively (Reznich, 2010). Student feedback should provide valuable information for teachers to address this key issue. In addition, students are the ones who experience the course and medical curriculum first hand. So, they should be able to provide information on the appropriateness of various teaching strategies employed on them. Thus, teachers should value student feedback in the process of course design or curriculum revision.

Assessment is also a pertinent part of education. The value of providing students with information in the guise of formative feedback obtained from assessment has been recognised as an effective assessment strategy that can enhance students' learning (Gronlund, 2003). Educators encourage medical teachers to provide more formative feedback to medical students and residents through the development of different types of workplace-based assessment (Norcini & Burch, 2007). Again, the benefits of feedback should not stop there. Having experienced the assessment first hand, students should be able to give feedback on how the assessment should be carried out.

There is some resistance to using student feedback to make changes in the curriculum or instruction. Some researchers have demonstrated that only a few items on the student rating forms relate directly to student achievement (Cohen, 1981; Feldman, 1989). Additionally, many teachers do not use the information obtained from student course evaluations to improve their teaching, as demonstrated from research findings revealing that student ratings of teaching practices via the course evaluation feedback shows no long-term improvement trend (L'Hommedieu, Menges, & Brinko, 1990; Lang & Kersting, 2007). Some teachers have expressed their resistance to using student feedback, based on the claims that student ratings are unreliable and the ratings favour teachers who entertain them over those who teach effectively. Some also claimed that student ratings were correlated with expected grades (Costin, Greenough, & Menges, 1971). Furthermore, there are concerns over the level of resources institutions invest in obtaining student feedback, especially when there is no evidence showing that teachers really use it to improve their instruction.

Despite some resistance, most educators would agree that student feedback is a valuable source of information that can help medical teachers improve their work in many areas, ranging from teaching strategies, course design, curriculum, and assessment approaches. Literature suggests that student feedback is at least as good as or even better than other alternative means of teaching evaluation (Greenwood & Ramagli, 1980). This chapter will describe how a medical school can obtain student feedback and how such information is used to improve teaching and learning practice. This chapter will provide a perspective on the use of student feedback in the context of Thai society. The chapter will do this through outlining experiences of using student feedback at the Faculty of Medicine, Siriraj Hospital, Mahidol University, Bangkok, Thailand.

Medical education in Thailand

This chapter will provide an insight into how student feedback is obtained and used in the Faculty of Medicine, Siriraj Hospital. In order to gain an understanding of how student feedback is utilised in this setting, first the educational context of the faculty will be described. Then, various aspects of the use of student feedback will be explained, including student feedback on individual teachers, student feedback on teaching strategies, student feedback on particular courses, student feedback on curricula, and student feedback on assessment. Also described in this chapter is the use of resident feedback to improve the training programme.

Medical schools in Thailand enrol applicants from high schools (Grade 12) without the requirement of a bachelor's degree. A medical degree takes six years of regular full-time study to complete. During their six-year period in medical school, students study for a total of 236 – 263 credits, which are divided up into three major sections. The first section is called premedical education, which is the first school year. During this period, students study in general education and basic sciences. The subjects studied during this period include physics, chemistry, biology, calculus, statistics, language, philosophy, and social science. The second section is called preclinical education, which are the second and third years. During this period, students study in subjects considered to be foundational to an understanding of the human body and diseases, without significant involvement in patient care. The subjects studied during this period include anatomy, physiology, biochemistry, pharmacology, microbiology, and pathology. The third section is called clinical education, which takes place during the last three years of school. During this period, students are rotated through various clinical departments, involving various teams of doctors that take care of patients. Their learning experience involves working in many departments, including internal medicine, surgery, paediatrics, obstetrics and gynaecology, and many others.

During the time that students study in medical school, they are also required to take a three-step national medical licensing examination. A medical school graduate who has successfully passed the medical licensing examination usually goes to work as a general practitioner in Thailand for a period of one to three years. Graduates intending to become medical specialists apply for a residency training position in the field of their interest. Residency training takes three to five years, depending on the specialty.

Thai culture differs in some respects from western cultures. These differences impact the thoughts and behaviours of students and teachers in many ways. Some notable cultural influences on the use of feedback should be clarified here. First, Thai culture emphasises the display of respect of the younger towards the elder (Cornwel-Smith & Gross, 2009). This tends to prohibit students from expressing their disagreement with teachers. Most students are reluctant to voice their dissatisfaction with teachers because they perceive such action as showing disrespect. Furthermore, Thais tend to focus on community or societal benefits more than personal gain. Students are taught not to make suggestions or comments in ways that would show that they value their own benefits more than the greater good of the community. Thais live in a geographical area with a relatively warm climate. Without harsh winter seasons, food can be grown and harvested throughout the year. This influences the psyche of Thai people, allowing them to be fairly laid back. Thai people tend not to want urgent or immediate changes, especially if making those changes would result in confrontation with authoritative figures. Due to all of the unique characteristics of Thai culture mentioned here, obtaining student feedback in the setting of a Thai medical school is a challenging task.

The Faculty of Medicine at Siriraj Hospital is the oldest and largest medical school in Thailand. It was founded in 1890. Currently, 292 students enrol into a doctor of medicine (MD) programme every year. The faculty provides residency training in almost all medical specialties, with around 1,000 residents and fellows working and studying in the hospital. In the following sections, some strategies that have been employed in the Faculty of Medicine, Siriraj Hospital in order to obtain student feedback in the context of Thai culture will be described. Undergraduate medical education will be discussed first, followed by postgraduate residency training.

Use of student feedback in undergraduate medical education

The following section provides a short discussion on the use of medical students' feedback in various aspects of medical education. Four levels of feedback on instruction will be discussed, including feedback on individual teachers, feedback on teaching strategies, feedback on a course, and feedback on a medical curriculum. Finally, the use of student feedback on assessment will be examined.

Student feedback on individual teachers

Student feedback on teachers' performance is not routinely required. Most medical teachers do not formally ask for student feedback on their teaching performance, except when it is required for academic promotion. Mahidol University has a requirement that students provide ratings of teachers' performance as a part of teaching quality evaluation at the time of academic promotion. Teaching performance ratings can be considered as formal feedback obtained from students. Some teachers regularly ask for students' ratings of their teaching performance, even when they are not applying for academic promotion. In the context of this teaching performance rating, individual students provide anonymous feedback on the following issues: (1) use of innovative teaching methods in order to make the lesson interesting; (2) providing additional resources for study; (3) providing opportunities for students to express their opinions; (4) skilled use of instructional media and equipment; (5) punctuality; (6) respectable personality; (7) use of polite language, and (8) dress code.

In addition to rating these eight aspects of teaching, students can also provide additional comments and suggestions at the bottom of the rating form. Some teachers consider this source of student feedback a valuable resource to help them improve their teaching skills. In some cases, improved ratings have been observed as teachers gradually adjust their teaching strategies to address student feedback.

The fact that the acquisition of student ratings of teaching performance is not a routine requirement of teaching reflects the influence of Thai culture on medical education. This shows a societal value that suppresses younger people in expressing their disagreement with senior staff members. Thus, the university allows faculty members to decide for themselves whether to be assessed by students in individual teaching sessions. Teachers who do not want to obtain this information can continue teaching as usual. On the other hand, teachers who are open-minded and want information from individual students can use the teaching performance ratings as guidance on the direction to improve their teaching skills. Only a small number of medical teachers regularly ask their students to provide teaching performance ratings. This could be for many reasons, such as a desire to limit the amount of paperwork, or a lack of recognition of the value of student feedback.

The anonymity of the ratings is very important in this setting, as Thai culture emphasises the display of respect to teachers and providing unsatisfactory ratings could be perceived as being disrespectful. With the imposition of rating anonymity, students participate in the teaching performance rating process at a rate of 85–100 per cent.

Student feedback on teaching strategies

In some subjects, medical teachers want to implement innovative teaching strategies. Although extensive literature reviews prior to implementing these innovative teaching strategies should have demonstrated their benefits, teachers never know whether using new approaches in a traditional medical school in a context of Thai culture will be appropriate. Many cultural considerations could prevent an innovative teaching method from working well in Thai culture, such as the unfamiliarity of students with an active learning environment, a reluctance to participate in activities in front of a large classroom, a lack of training in critical thinking and problem solving in high schools, and students' shyness in expressing opinions that may contradict their teachers. Thus, medical teachers who employ new teaching strategies routinely seek student feedback.

An example of the use of student feedback in the context of utilising innovative teaching techniques is the recent implementation of team-based learning (Michaelsen, 1983) in a class of fourth-year medical students in the Department of Surgery (Michaelsen, Parmelee, McMahon, & Levine, 2008). Despite having research evidence of the effectiveness of this teaching strategy, the department sought students' perspectives on this active-learning approach. Thus, at the last session of team-based learning, students were asked to provide ratings on 15 aspects of learning and answer 5 open-ended questions. The 15 issues that students provided ratings of were: (1) usefulness of the studied content; (2) good understanding of the taught content; (3) use of the active learning strategy; (4) enjoyable learning experience; (5) development of team working skills; (6) usefulness of the required reading materials; (7) the appropriateness of the amount of reading materials; (8) ability to finish all the assigned reading materials before class; (9) the adequacy of time provided for an individual test; (10) the adequacy of time provided for a team-based test; (11) the adequacy of time provided for team-based application exercises; (12) the appropriateness of the test content; (13) the complexity of the cases provided in the application exercise; (14) the quality of feedback from the teacher, and (15) the recommendation to use team-based learning. The five open-ended questions were: (1) the most useful topic learned; (2) what was most impressive about their experience; (3) what should be changed; (4) other topics for team-based learning, and (5) other comments and suggestions.

Based on student feedback obtained at the end of team-based learning, the details of the instructional strategy were reviewed and some changes made to improve students' experience in this teaching method. A few students indicated that they could not finish the reading materials before the class. Thus, the list of reading materials was revised to reduce the reading workload among students. A few students also complained about the inadequacy of the allotted time for group tests. A revision of testing time was made to provide students with more time to discuss their answers in groups. Some students revealed that they did not have enough time to elaborate on all critical issues related to the cases.

The number of cases given to students during the application exercise was reduced from four to three to decrease students' stress. Student feedback is obviously critical in pointing out many areas for instructional improvement when implementing a new teaching strategy.

Student feedback on a course

Medical teachers actively seek student feedback in order to improve their learning experience in every course. This includes both verbal and written feedback. An example is an approach taken in the Department of Surgery, which provides courses to fourth-, fifth-, and sixth- year medical students. In every course offered by the Department of Surgery, medical teachers arrange a meeting with students for three hours of an afternoon about midway through the course and run a session entitled 'ventilation hours'. During this session, teachers actively ask for feedback from medical students. Medical students describe their learning experience in the department so far, and provide both positive and negative feedback to teachers. Many suggestions from students address important learning needs, which teachers subsequently bring to the attention of the educational committee of the department so that changes can be made to the organisation of the course. Some examples of changes that the department has made based on suggestions from students through the 'ventilation hours' include rearrangement of the surgical services that students experience during ward rounds, re-organising the system for assigning patients to students to see and write reports on, improving the condition of the doctors' room where medical students and surgical residents rest during their on-call duties, and revising job descriptions of medical students and residents.

However, there have also been some suggestions from students that were not appropriate and might not result in learning improvement. Examples of these suggestions include: making changes in clinical services in ways that have previously created problems, reducing students' workload in a way that might compromise patients safety and reduce important learning experiences, and some forms of system change that would require significant financial investment. Teachers always take this opportunity to explain why the course has been organised in the way it was and why it should not be changed in ways suggested by students. This two-way communication between students and teachers helps students feel engaged in the course, and helps make the course organisation more transparent to all stakeholders. Such student-teacher interaction is a valuable learning experience for students. It provides students with legitimate peripheral participation, as required for learning to occur according to situated learning theory (Lave & Wenger, 1991).

In the surgical course offered to sixth-year medical students, learning experience is obtained through work in affiliated hospitals located in other parts of the country (some in the city, but many in rural areas). Medical teachers also actively seek student feedback in these settings. Surgical faculty members take turns visiting students in the affiliated hospitals. During the visits, students are asked to describe their learning experience in the affiliated hospital, provide feedback, and give suggestions on how teachers can help them gain better learning experience in affiliated hospitals. Some suggestions can be implemented immediately. During the visits, surgical faculty members discuss the accommodation of student needs with the doctors who are in charge of the educational mission of that particular hospital. Some suggestions are reasonable and might help improve student learning, but cannot be implemented immediately. Visiting surgical faculty members bring back these suggestions to the educational committee of the department to discuss the possibility of making changes for future groups of students. After elaborated discussion of the issue, the educational committee makes a decision whether to implement the changes as suggested by students. Some notable examples of educational changes that have been made through such processes include: changes in the list of affiliated hospitals for students to obtain their experience in; the adjustment of the system to allow online access to medical journals to students and doctors from affiliated hospitals, and improved communication between doctors at affiliated hospitals and faculty members at the Department of Surgery.

At the end of all the courses offered by the Department of Surgery, all students are asked to provide written feedback to the department. As part of this feedback, students rate their satisfaction with various learning activities provided by the department, and also write comments and suggestions freely and anonymously. The information obtained from this student feedback is summarised in a report. All the teachers involved in teaching the course are informed about this student feedback in a monthly meeting of the educational committee and through a written report sent to every division in the department.

The information obtained through both verbal and written feedback collected from students has helped surgical faculty members adjust the surgical course in a way that better serves the needs of medical students. All the departments that offer courses to medical students in this faculty perform similar activities to evaluate the course and collate suggestions on ways of improving student learning.

Student feedback on a medical curriculum

At the time of graduation, medical students have seen the curriculum completely and are in a good position to suggest ways of improving it. The Faculty of Medicine at Siriraj Hospital always arranges meeting sessions with graduates shortly before their final ceremony. In this meeting, medical teachers ask graduates to give their opinions on the curriculum that they have experienced and ways in which the faculty can improve it. Most of the comments in this session are positive, indicating the usefulness of various subjects graduates have been taught during their studies. However, there are also some suggestions given by the graduates on how to modify the curriculum. For example, which topics should be emphasised more, what types of clinical experience students require more of, and which teaching strategies they would like to see more of in the curriculum. As the amount of time in this feedback session is limited and it is impossible for everyone to voice their opinions, the faculty also provides questionnaires to graduates to fill in during these sessions. In the questionnaire, graduates are asked to rate their achievements in various medical competencies now that they've completed the programme, and provide satisfaction ratings on various aspects of the medical curriculum. The graduates are also asked for feedback on various issues using open-ended questions, such as their impression of the curriculum, their opinions on clinical skills teaching in the faculty and in affiliated hospitals, their suggestions on how to assess their learning, and their quality of experience in the faculty. Generally, there is a high level of graduate participation in this survey, with a questionnaire return rate of about 80 per cent.

Medical teachers take the information obtained from graduates seriously. The Faculty of Medicine, Siriraj Hospital summarises the information from these sessions and from the questionnaires every year. The Office of Undergraduate Education incorporates this information with feedback obtained from other stakeholders, including parents and bosses of graduates, into annual reports. Data from previous years in compared to highlight trends in graduates' satisfaction with the curriculum.

When a medical curriculum is due to be reviewed, medical teachers always value current students and graduates' input. The representatives of medical students and recent graduates are always asked to provide their perspectives on what changes the faculty should make to the curriculum. Currently, the faculty is in the process of major curriculum revision in response to the many skills required for the 21st century workforce (Bellanca & Brandt, 2010; Kay & Greenhill, 2012), the Medical Council of Thailand's changes in the core medical competencies (The Medical Council of Thailand, 2012), and the development of the Asian economic community. In this process of curricular revision, current students and recent graduates are asked to provide feedback on what they would want in a new curriculum. The faculty invited representatives of students and recent graduates to voice their opinions in major curricular revision meetings. The state of the new medical curriculum will certainly be influenced by feedback from students and graduates.

Student feedback on assessment

Assessment is an essential component of a curriculum. When properly designed and appropriately used, assessment procedures can contribute to more effective instruction and greater student learning (Gronlund, 2003). With new developments in the field of assessment (such as computer-based tests, workplace-based assessment, portfolios), many assessment approaches that medical teachers employ in the curriculum may need to be changed from time to time. Although these changes are made based on a careful consideration of scientific evidence, medical teachers cannot neglect the importance of students' first-hand experience with the implementation of new assessment approaches. Students can provide valuable information about the appropriateness of the assessment procedures that they go through. At the Faculty of Medicine, Siriraj Hospital, student feedback is always obtained when new assessment approaches are implemented. An example is in making the transition from a traditional paper-based examination to a computerised examination. The change was first made in a modified essay question examination in January 2010. At the end of the examination, students were asked to provide written feedback on various aspects of the examination. The first part of the form asked students to rate their satisfaction with aspects of the examination, such as: the appropriateness of the examination format; the appropriateness of the number of test items; the appropriateness of the time provided; the difficulty level; the quality of the computer system; the clarity of the photos and text display; the appropriateness of the testing room, and the appropriateness of the date scheduled for the exam. The second part of the form was an open-ended question asking students for their suggestions about how the test should be administered. About 97 per cent of students participated in this survey. The participating students provided valuable information through their feedback. Their feedback has helped the faculty gradually improve the testing experience of students. For example, students suggested extending resting time between test items, and a change in the method of signalling to students when the testing time was up.

With positive responses obtained from students on computerised modified essay questions, the faculty then made the transition to computerisation on a multiple-choice examination in February 2011. Because implementing a computerised multiple-choice examination required individual students to navigate the test on a computer by themselves, making the changes was carefully planned. Students were asked to provide feedback even before implementing the new computerised system. A simulated test was developed and posted online. All students were asked to download the test and try it. After they had tried working on this simulated test, students provided feedback by rating their satisfaction with numerous aspects, including the instruction, ease of navigation, font size and style, the use of menus, display design, the colour of backgrounds, the colour of text, and the amount of time provided to do the test. Open-ended questions were also employed to ask for their suggestions. A lot of valuable information was obtained, which has helped the school modify the test administration in ways designed to satisfy most students. When the faculty actually administered the computerised test, students were asked again for their feedback at the end of the exam. This end-of-exam survey contained 27 items for which students provided satisfaction ratings, encompassing four aspects of the exam, including the computer system, the quality of the test, the test administration, and the overall organisation of the test. At the bottom of the form, students were also asked for their suggestions. Based on their input, the software and test administration procedures have been modified over the years to improve the exam experience of students.

As mentioned earlier, Thais usually do not favour sudden changes. The transition from a paper-based examination to a computerised test administration in only a short period, as described here, also encountered some resistance from students, because some felt that this would have a negative impact on their test scores. However, one factor that helped make the change possible was the teachers' acceptance of student feedback. Students could see the effort teachers made in seeking their suggestions on how to improve their test experience. The adjustment of testing conditions in a way that students suggested was clear evidence of teachers' acknowledgement of student feedback.

The use of resident feedback in postgraduate training

Another group of learners that medical teachers cannot overlook are those in the residency training programme. They acquire their knowledge, skills, and attitudes while providing medical services under the supervision of medical teachers. This group of learners is more mature. They have more knowledge, skills, and experience than undergraduate students. Their opinions should be a valuable source of information for medical teachers who are interested in improving the training programme. All residency training programmes in the Faculty of Medicine, Siriraj Hospital continuously solicit the feedback of residents. An example is a general surgery residency programme. The Department of Surgery obtains residents' feedback through various means, including informal discussion, scheduled meeting, and end-of-rotation written feedback.

Because residents work closely with medical teachers, there are always opportunities to discuss various issues besides work. Many medical teachers form mentoring relationships with their residents. In the mentoring process, a teacher not only directs what a resident should do, but also listens to what a resident thinks about the training programme. A good mentor actively listens to their mentee's feedback on various aspects of the course, some of which will benefit the mentor or the training programme (Kay & Hinds, 2009). This source of information helps guide medical teachers in finding ways to improve the training programme.

It is typical practice for a programme director to schedule a regular meeting with representatives of surgical residents to discuss their well-being and to solve any issues that come up during work. During these scheduled meeting sessions, programme directors often receive a lot of feedback that they can then use to inform the department about what the residents would want.

The most comprehensive source of feedback obtained from surgical residents is written feedback obtained at the end of every rotation. Every resident receives a questionnaire at the end of every rotation (rotations range between four and eight weeks). These questionnaires ask residents to provide satisfaction ratings on ten aspects of clinical experience of that particular rotation, including the amount of knowledge gained, the number of surgical procedures practiced, the quantity of academic activities, the format and content of academic activities, the amount of work being assigned, the work environment, the variety of cases, the attention of attending staff towards residents' well-being, the opportunity to get involved in making decisions about the cases, and the quality of teachers. At the end of the questionnaire, there is an open space in which a resident can provide any comments or feedback related to their experience in that particular clinical rotation. The department continuously monitors the quality of training programmes using this resident feedback. Many critical issues related to training and the quality of life of residents have been detected from this resident feedback form and led to additional investigations and modification of the training programme.

Conclusion

Feedback obtained from learners, either at undergraduate or postgraduate level, is a valuable source of information that teachers who are interested in improving the clinical learning experience of students should not neglect. In this chapter, the various uses of learners' feedback in one medical faculty in Thailand were described. These few examples described how feedback is obtained and how it is used to improve the medical curriculum in various aspects, including individual teachers, teaching strategies, courses, assessment approaches, and even the entire curriculum. The experiences outlined in this chapter will hopefully help inspire other teachers to actively seek learners' feedback and use it to enhance medical teaching and learning.

References

Bellanca, J., & Brandt, R. (2010). *21st Century Skills: Rethinking How Students Learn*. Bloomington, IN: Solution Tree Press.

Cohen, P. A. (1981). Student ratings of instruction and student achievement: a meta-analysis of multisection validity studies. *Review of Educational Research, 51*(3), 281–309.

Coles, C. (1998). How students learn: the process of learning. In B. Jolly & L. Rees (Eds.), *Medical Education in the Millennium* (pp. 63–82). New York: Oxford University Press.

Cornwel-Smith, P., & Gross, J. (2009). *Very Thai: Everyday popular culture, 2nd ed.* Bangkok: River Books Press.

Costin, F., Greenough, W. T., & Menges, R. J. (1971). Student ratings of college teaching: reliability, validity, and usefulness. *Review of Educational Research, 41*(5), 511–535.

Ericsson, K. A. (2006). The influence of experience and deliberate practice on the development of superior expert performance. In K. A. Ericsson, N. Charness, P. J. Feltovich & R. R. Hoffman (Eds.), *The Cambridge Handbook of Expertise and Expert Performance* (pp. 685–706). Cambridge, UK: Cambridge University Press.

Ericsson, K. A., Krampe, R. T., & Tesch-Romer, C. (1993). The role of deliberate practice in the acquisition of expert performance. *Psychological Review, 100*(3), 363–406.

Feldman, K. A. (1989). The association between student ratings of specific instructional dimensions and student achievement: refining and extending the synthesis of data from multisection validity studies. *Research in Higher Education, 30*, 583–645.

Greenwood, G. E., & Ramagli, H. J., Jr. (1980). Alternatives to student ratings of college teaching. *Journal of Higher Education, 51*(6), 673–684.

Gronlund, N. E. (2003). *Assessment of Student Achievement, 7th ed.* Boston, MA: Pearson Education.

Kay, D., & Hinds, R. (2009). *A Practical Guide to Mentoring: How to Help Others Achieve their Goals, 4th ed.* Oxford: How To Books.

Kay, K., & Greenhill, V. (2012). *The Leader's Guide to 21st Century Education: 7 Steps for Schools and Districts.* Boston, MA: Pearson Education.

L'Hommedieu, R., Menges, R. J., & Brinko, K. T. (1990). Methodological explanations for the modest effects of feedback from student ratings. *Journal of Educational Psychology, 82*(2), 232–241.

Lang, J. W., & Kersting, M. (2007). Regular feedback from student ratings of instruction: do college teachers improve their ratings in the long run? *Instructional Science, 35*, 187–205.

Lave, J., & Wenger, E. (1991). *Situated learning: legitimate peripheral participation.* New York: Cambridge University Press.

Michaelsen, L. K. (1983). Team learning in large classes. In C. Bouton & R. Y. Garth (Eds.), *Learning in Groups* (pp. 13–22). San Francisco, CA: Jossey-Bass.

Michaelsen, L. K., Parmelee, D. X., McMahon, K. K., & Levine, R. E. (2008). *Team-based Learning for Health Professions Education: a Guide to Using Small Groups for Improving Learning.* Sterling, VA: Stylus publishing.

Norcini, J., & Burch, V. (2007). Workplace-based assessment as an educational tool: AMEE guide no. 31. *Medical Teacher, 29*, 855–871.

Reznich, C. B. (2010). Designing a course. In W. B. Jeffries & K. N. Huggett (Eds.), *An Introduction to Medical Teaching* (pp. 123–142). Dodrecht: Springer.

Sargeant, J., & Mann, K. (2010). Feedback in medical education: Skills for improving learner performance. In P. Cantillon & D. Wood (Eds.), *ABC of Learning and Teaching in Medicine* (pp. 29–32). Oxford, UK: Wiley-Blackwell.

The Medical Council of Thailand. (2012). *Professional Standards for Medical Practitioners 2012.* Bangkok.

Van de Ridder, J. M. M., Stokking, K. M., McGaghie, W. C., & Cate, O. T. J. (2008). What is feedback in clinical education? *Medical Education, 42*, 189–197.

Student Feedback in Medical and Health Sciences: an Indian Perspective

Rita Sood,
Department of Medicine, All India Institute of Medical Sciences

Tejinder Singh,
Department of Paediatrics, Christian Medical College

Abstract: Feedback from students about the effectiveness of teaching and relevance of curricula is well recognised as a tool to help improve the quality of courses. Around the world, it is accepted as an essential part of the educational process and is considered vital in improving the effectiveness of teaching. Along with other measures, it is also considered a useful tool for the evaluation of academic staff.

This chapter presents a case study of how student feedback is utilised in health sciences in the Indian context. Despite the recognised value of student feedback for continuous quality improvement of courses, it is not a regular feature utilised in health science in most Indian universities.

Keywords: Student feedback; faculty evaluation; teacher effectiveness; health sciences; validity; reliability

Use of student feedback for evaluation of faculty (SEF)

Feedback from students about the effectiveness of teaching and the relevance of curricula is well-recognised and accepted the world over as a key factor in improving the quality of courses. Over time, student ratings have increasingly been used to assist in decisions on personnel, such as hiring, retention, tenure, promotion, salary increases, awards, etc. Since the 1970s, student ratings of teaching have become commonplace in American colleges and universities and have become synonymous with faculty evaluation (Seldin, 1999). Since student ratings provide only one source of feedback on teaching effectiveness, their use for such decision making can be problematic. When used for making such decisions, student ratings need to be used in combination with other evidence of teaching effectiveness. These include peer ratings, self-assessment, alumni ratings, course documents, students' performance and progress, and teaching portfolios.

Common criticisms and perceptions of SEF

It does not come as a surprise that there is sharp disagreement within the academic community about the use of student ratings as a measure of an instructor's performance. Concerns have been expressed about the use of SEF in judging faculty performance and in decisions made by promotion and tenure committees. Haskell (1997) makes a strong argument against the use and misuse of SEF in tenure and other administrative decisions. He focusses on the possible impact of SEF on professors' academic freedom and on the quality of instruction, as well as concerns regarding the consequences of evaluation, especially the misuse of evaluation results and the legal consequences that could result. He cites a number of examples suggesting SEF can be used to shape faculty behaviour, curricular content, and the kind of faculty that are retained in the programmes.

Haskell's concerns about these points are also shared by other researchers in the field (Wines & Lan, 2006). There are numerous statements by faculty members in the research literature arguing that SEF is an infringement of academic freedom. These statements contend that SEF is prima facie evidence of administrative intrusion into the classroom, and are often used as an instrument of intimidation forcing conformity to politically correct standards (Young, 1993), are responsible for a considerable amount of grade inflation (Greenwald, 1996 & 1997) and, when used for promotions and tenure, become a potent means for manipulating the behaviour of academics (Stone, 1995). Haskell (1998) argues that SEF creates an educational conflict of interest between faculty and students, impacting on the quality of instruction.

In addition to controversy over lenient grading by teachers, an overemphasis on students' emotional response to entertaining teachers, regardless of educational content of the class, has been the basis for criticism of the legitimacy of student evaluations (Naftulin et al, 1973; Ware & Williams, 1975). Usually, concerns about student feedback on the curricular process are related to the fact (and sometimes the presumption) that students may be unaware of what is ultimately expected of them, and their feedback may lead to erroneous evaluation of some parts of curriculum. Some feel that these evaluations may be unfocussed and undisciplined and may be based on faculty popularity or entertainment value (Theall & Franklin, 1991; Seldin, 1993).

In India too, quite often faculty members are apprehensive about student ratings and student evaluation is viewed with skepticism. Teachers are sometimes concerned about the prospect of being evaluated by students. They often perceive students not to be mature enough to judge teachers' teaching capabilities. On the other hand, students fear that any adverse ratings they give teachers may jeopardise their future careers.

Key points on the utility of student feedback

The following points emerge regarding making full use of student feedback as a quality improvement tool (Cashin, 1999; Theall & Franklin, 2001; Seldin, 1993; Kulik, 2001):

1. The purpose, use, and utility of student ratings should be discussed with all stakeholders. Special emphasis needs to be placed on what is going to be done with the data. Student ratings should be only one of several data sources on teaching performance.

2. Academics need to be informed of the scientific basis of student ratings, specially related to its validity, reliability, and stability.

3. Basic training in the interpretation of such data needs to be provided.

4. The questionnaire need not be too extensive, but should comprehensively cover the teaching behaviour.

5. Survey questions should focus on observable teaching behaviours only, with several open-ended questions.

6. The best time to administer questionnaires is early in the semester so that teachers can adjust their teachings. They should cover all semesters and all courses.

7. If less than 75 per cent of the students have answered the questionnaire, additional information should be sought before making any judgements.

8. Scores should be available to teachers along with a comparison (maybe the scores of their peers) so that they can contextualise their ratings.

9. Teachers should have the opportunity to discuss scores with peers/ administration in a non-threatening atmosphere.

10. More extensive research ought to be conducted on student ratings.

The authors believe that gathering feedback from students can be a helpful way to get a glimpse into how they are experiencing a course – what is working and what is not working for them – and, thus, offers suggestions to make the course better. It is important to consider carefully what students say about the course and first consider positive feedback. It is too easy to get swayed by negative comments and negative feedback is often taken so personally. It is easy to get defensive and quickly blame the process (Anonymous, 2013a).

It is important to let students know what influence their feedback has. Students appreciate knowing that a teacher has carefully considered what they have said. It is also important to let students know what proactive steps they can take. For example, if students say they are often confused, they should be invited to ask questions more often. (Anonymous, 2013b).

The following section presents a case study concerning utilising student feedback in health sciences in the Indian context.

Some background in Indian medical education

India has the largest medical education system in the world with 381 medical schools in the country at present. There has been a rapid proliferation of the number of medical schools over the last two decades, particularly in the private sector (Sood & Adkoli, 2000; Sood, 2008). Students are eligible to enter into medical school immediately after their schooling of 12 years (10+2), through a highly competitive knowledge-based entrance examination. The Medical Council of India (MCI), the regulatory body, is required to approve any significant reforms in the medical curricula. The recognition process by the council focusses largely on the infrastructure and the human resources required, and little on the process and quality of education and outcomes. Though largely governed by the council, health science universities individually have variable sets of regulations for their affiliated medical schools. The All India Institute of Medical Sciences, where one of the authors works, is an autonomous institute established by an act of parliament. It works independently of the MCI and awards its own degrees (www.aiims.ac.in). The departments have relative freedom to innovate, keeping in mind the objectives of the training programmes.

Cultural and contextual issues regarding use of student feedback in India

For academics to receive feedback from students about teaching and use it effectively for improvement, it is important that there is an atmosphere of trust between teachers and students. In India, in most health-related professional educational institutions, teachers are often not convinced that students are mature enough to rate their teaching and give honest feedback, and also are generally not prepared to accept criticism of their teaching. This became apparent to the authors through personal observations.

The medical teacher-student relationship in India is still guided by the traditional colonial philosophy where the teacher is regarded as supreme, and can influence the trajectory of a student's career. A number of questionable practices related to the giving of marks for internal assessment, for example, have been reported (Singh et al, 2012). Students, therefore, find it more convenient to keep their opinions to themselves rather than to risk their careers. Students need to be convinced that their feedback is valued and must be assured of anonymity. Creating a climate of openness and transparency must precede the process of collecting and using student feedback effectively. Honest feedback will not be obtained in a hostile environment where a student fears repercussions for criticism (Afonso et al, 2005).

Current use of student feedback in medical and health professional education in India

As mentioned above, regular use of student feedback to improve the effectiveness of teaching is not practised in most medical and other health professional schools in India, and the subject has not gained favour with most educators.

However, there are a number of reports published on student evaluation of innovative curricula and courses within the Indian context (Abraham, 2008; Bhowmick, 2009; Shankar, 2012). These are generally helpful in disseminating these innovations and in the institutionalisation of good practices. Obtaining feedback from students can be used as a motivator for the improvement of teaching. One of the authors of this chapter obtained student feedback on all teachers of basic science. The individual, anonymous results of other teachers were shown to the teachers and no further input was provided. The process was repeated after six months with the same cohort of teachers and students, and a significant increase in the ratings was noticed. This phenomenon of change in behaviour on being observed, often called the 'Hawthorne effect', can be a very useful input by itself (Singh et al, 1991).

Although student feedback is not a regular feature at the institutes where the authors work, some departments at the medical school of the first author (such as the Department of Physiology and the College of Nursing) regularly use student feedback to enhance the quality of teaching, although they use it in different ways. Experiences with the use of student feedback are given below.

Department of Physiology

Obtaining feedback from students by faculty members has been a regular feature in the Department of Physiology, AIIMS, for a number of years. The feedback is informal and is obtained through structured questionnaires that are filled out by the students after the completion of a module (a lecture series). Individual teachers have the option of obtaining feedback after every lecture if they so desire.

The feedback is usually sought on the following aspects of the teaching-learning exercise, in the format illustrated below:

1. Adequate course content covered;

2. Whether aligned to stated objectives;

3. Manner of teaching was helpful in understanding the topic;

4. Delivery of content (teaching methodology):

    a. Aroused interest in the topic;

    b. Speed of delivery of content was optimal (Mention fast/slow);

c. Important concepts reinforced/repeated;

d. Student questions included;

e. Responded well to student queries;

f. The session was interactive;

g. Timed well to cover the entire topic;

h. Summarized the topic at the end;

5. Use of audio-visual aids:

a. A-V aids used: Yes (OHP/LCD/Black/White board) / No / Not Applicable

b. If yes,

    i.   The A-V aid was optimally used

    ii.   Quality of material presented was good

    iii. Explanations were offered for projected concepts

    iv. Interaction was encouraged

    v.   The material recourses were shared/handouts distributed

6. Any other comments

The responses of the students are obtained on a Likert rating scale (1 = Strongly Agree, 2 = Agree, 3 = Neutral, 4 = Disagree and 5 = Strongly Disagree) for the first 5 items, except where a Yes/No response or written comments are required. Students are asked to write their comments on anything they wish to write about the session/faculty member/scheduling/infrastructure etc. while responding to item 6, and can turn the sheet over or add an extra sheet if required.

The main objective of obtaining student feedback is to render the teaching-learning program more effective, consistent, current, and contemporary. It is also meant to assist faculty members in improving the quality of their teaching by incorporating relevant changes in their teaching styles/strategies to better engage the students and meet their expectations. In addition to the above, the feedback often provides avenues to institute corrective measures in the planning, scheduling, and alignment of the teaching programme to overcome shortcomings that have been identified as genuine. For example, if the majority of the students feel that alteration in the sequence of modules taught would help in their examinations, or if the employment of a specific A-V aid for a specific sub-topic would improve comprehension. Frequently, interesting comments related to personal habits, mannerisms, appearance and turnout of the faculty members were encountered. These have generally been taken on board by academics. The students are usually highly observant, attentive, and sincere in their feedback and comments. The students can comment openly, because they are given the option of identifying themselves or remaining anonymous, by not writing their names or roll numbers on the feedback forms. The feedback forms are retained by the faculty members and the option of sharing the outcome or discussing the feedback in toto or in part with peers, or with the head of the department, is available to them. Overall, the practice of obtaining student feedback and the results of the process has been appreciated by students and faculty members alike, and the department has benefitted immensely from it.

College of Nursing

The postgraduate nursing programme (MSc) initiated in the year 2004 by the College of Nursing, AIIMS, is a two-year programme, with teaching carried out by seven sub-specialty departments. Feedback from students about the programme and faculty teaching is obtained on a regular basis.

For an overall evaluation of teaching in the discipline, feedback from students is obtained regarding coverage of topics, organisation of individual lectures, clarity and pace of lectures, use of audio-visual aids, interactivity during the sessions, and additional efforts by the faculty to facilitate understanding of the subject matter. For evaluation of individual teachers' performances, feedback from students is obtained regarding most of these parameters.

Utilisation of feedback

Faculty members are provided with feedback from students about their individual performance, to help them improve in the desired areas. The feedback from students is also taken into account for curricular modification after discussions in the curriculum committee meetings. Student feedback has been reported to be very useful in improving this programme which has become apparent in the authors' personal communication with college teaching staff.

Manipal University Experience

Manipal University of Health Sciences is one of the oldest private universities in the country and now has many branches outside India. Though largely regulated by the MCI, it has adopted many innovative educational practices over the years (www.manipal.edu). At the Manipal University of Health Sciences, regular feedback is obtained from students for enhancing teaching effectiveness and teacher evaluation (authors' personal communication). The feedback obtained from students is utilised to enhance the effectiveness of teaching by individual teachers, as well as to help evaluate departmental and institutional effectiveness and for faculty appraisal and rewards. How this is done is outlined below.

Individual: The University utilises an evaluation form which takes into consideration essential dimensions of effective teaching such as enthusiasm, organisation of content, group interaction, and breadth of coverage of a topic. It also probes teacher rapport with students and use of technology in curriculum delivery. Space is also provided for open-ended and other additional items to be included as and when required by the faculty. This form is made available for the entire teaching faculty and they are encouraged to use the same during the delivery of courses and for collecting feedback from learners in order to enhance their teaching effectiveness.

Departmental: A modified version of the aforesaid form is used here. Besides looking for the essential factors cited above, it also ranks the faculty in a department based on student feedback. The survey is carried out anonymously and by people who are not directly or indirectly involved with the course. Results are available to the head of the department and often used in the annual appraisal of staff. Staff have access to this information if required. This form also features questions that are open-ended and allow students to provide input on aspects of the curriculum, including delivery and assessment.

Institutional: This provides an overall evaluation of the course. Besides course content and organisation, it also looks into factors that contribute to the educational environment. Student feedback in the form of ratings is also conducted at institutional level, and is used in the conferring of good teacher awards instituted for the recognition of teaching excellence, which includes a citation, plaque, and cash award. In medical schools, one award is instituted per 100 students for each phase: preclinical, para-clinical, and clinical. Feedback is collected anonymously.

Prospects of using student feedback effectively in India

Student feedback is only one mechanism of collecting feedback for improving teaching programmes. It is essential that it be combined with other sources of feedback from teachers, peers, administrators, etc. to improve the validity and reliability of this data. Institutions must decide in advance what purposes the data will be used for. Teachers need to be made aware of literature on student feedback to improve acceptance of this method and to assist them in using it effectively. Concerns which make teachers averse to student feedback need to be discussed openly, and attempts must be made to address their apprehensions. They must be satisfied about the way this modality is used and must be aware of the utility, validity, and reliability of student feedback. It may be useful to issue centralised guidance about using student feedback as a modality. Uniform questionnaires may make interpretation easier.

Given initial resistance from academics to student feedback, it is essential to proceed gradually. One way of approaching this issue is to make the results of evaluation available to individual teachers. They can see their own scores as well as the scores received by their peers. A mechanism to help academics who get poor ratings must be in place. The experience of the second author with student feedback showed that repeating the exercise after six months resulted in improvement in the scores. Although scores alone may not be truly representative of better teaching, it can be argued that simply making teachers aware of the fact that students are observing their performance has a positive effect. It is imperative to provide an opportunity for teachers to discuss scores with peers/administration in a non-threatening atmosphere. Seldin (1984), one of the strongest advocates of the validity of SEF, warns that the confidentiality of the data is important. If data is shared, it must be with the consent and at the discretion of the appraised staff.

Recently, the Indian University Grants Commission (UGC) has issued instructions to all universities to collect student feedback on teachers and lecturers (teaching quality). However, an environment which is not open and where there is a lack of trust leads to skepticism among academics and fear among students. The National Assessment and Accreditation Council (NAAC), which is a national body involved with accreditation of educational institutions in India, uses student feedback as one of the criteria for accreditation. However, accreditation by the NAAC is not mandatory for institutions of higher education.

Role of faculty development

It is not enough to simply diagnose the situation by using scales. An important issue is to provide development advice so that teachers can improve their specific practices and behaviours. Theall and Franklin (1991) stated that when rating information is coupled with knowledgeable assistance, improvement can result.

The negative perspective on the value of student feedback among Indian academics stems from a lack of knowledge and misconceptions about the validity and reliability of this tool in improving the quality of teaching. Many teachers and administrators in India, and also in other countries, lack knowledge about the utility of student feedback, and this correlates significantly with negative opinion on the value of student feedback (Theall and Franklin, 2001). Academic development initiatives need to consider this as an important aspect of educational development.

Conclusion

Although student feedback is not widely accepted and practiced in Indian health sciences education, its role is being increasingly recognised as a part of continuous quality improvement in education. There are select centres utilising student feedback for evaluating new educational programmes, as well as for measuring teaching effectiveness and improving teaching and learning programmes. These practices need to be replicated and there is an urgent need for their growing ubiquity in the area of academic development within the Indian context.

Acknowledgements

We gratefully acknowledge the contributions of Dr Nalin Mehta, associate professor, Department of Physiology, Dr Sandhya Gupta, lecturer, College of Nursing, All India Institute of Medical Sciences, New Delhi, and Dr Ciraj Ali Mohammad, deputy director, Manipal Centre for Professional and Personal Development, Manipal University, for sharing experiences of student feedback from their institutions.

References

Abraham, R., Ramnarayan, K., Vinod, P. & Torke, S. (2008). Students' perceptions of learning environment in an Indian Medical School, *BMC Medical Education*, 8:20. doi10,1186/1472-6920-8-20. Available: *http://www.biomedcentral.com/1472-6920/8/20*

Abrami, P.C. (2001). Improving judgements about teaching effectiveness using teacher rating forms. *New Directions for Institutional Research*, 109, 59–88.

Afonso, N.M, Cardazo, L.J., Mascarenhas-Oswald, A.J., Aranha, A.N.F. & Shah, C. (2005). Are anonymous evaluations a better assessment of faculty teaching performance? A comparative analysis of open and anonymous evalution processes. *Fam Med*, 37 (1), 43–47.

All India Institute of Medical Sciences, New Delhi. Info available at: *www.aiims.ac.in*.

Anonymous (2013a). (Rose's TKT. Assessment for learning. Accessed from *http://rosalia89.edublogs.org/2012/05/17/assessment-for-learning/* on 2nd October 2013).

Anonymous (2013b). (Rose's TKT). Back talk … in the classroom. Accessed from *http://rosalia89.edublogs.org/2012/06/27/back-talk-in-the-classroom/* on 2nd October 2013.

Arreola, R.E. (1994). *Developing a Comprehensive Faculty Evaluation System*. Boston: Anker.

Bhowmick, K., Mukhopadhyay, M., Chakraborty, S., Sen, P.K., Chakraborty, I. (2009). Assessment of perception of first professional MBBS students in India about a teaching learning activity in biochemistry. *South East Asian Journal of Medical Education*, 3(2) 27–34.

Boice, R. (1992). *The New Faculty Member – Supporting and Fostering Professional Development*. San Francisco: Jossey Bass.

Cashin, W.E. (1989). Defining and evaluating college teaching. *IDEA Paper no 21 (21)*.

Cashin, W.E. (1995). Student ratings of teaching: the research revisited. *(IDEA paper No. 32)* Manhattan, Kansas State University, Centre for Faculty Evaluation and Development, pp. 1–9.

Cashin, W.E. (1999). Student ratings of teachers – uses and misuses. In: Seldin, P & Hutchings, P (Eds), *Changing Practices in Evaluating Teaching: a Practical Guide to Improved Faculty Performance and Promotion / Tenure Decisions*. (pp. 25–44). Anker: Bolton.

Centra, J.A. (1987). *Determing Faculty Effectiveness*. San Francisco: Jossey Bass.

Chen, Y. & Hoshower, L.B. (2003). Student evaluation of teaching effectiveness: an assessment of student perception and motivation. *Assessment & Evaluation in Higher Education*, 28(1), 71–88.

Cohen, P.A. (1981). Student ratings of instruction and student achievement: a meta analysis of multisection validity studies. *Review of Educational Research*, 51(3) 281–309.

Downing, S.M. (2003). Validity – on the meaningful interpretation of assessment data. *Medical Education*, 37, 830–837.

Feldman, K.A. (1989b). Instructional effectiveness of college teachers as judged by teachers themselves, current and former students, colleagues, administrators and external (neutral) observers. *Research in Higher Education, 30(2)*, 137–194.

Frey, P.W. (1979). The Dr Fox effect and its implications. *Instructional Evaluation, 3*, 1–5.

Greenwald, A.G. (1996). *Applying social psychology to reveal a major (but correctable) flaw in student evaluation of teaching.* Paper presented at the Annual meeting, University of Washington, March 1.

Greenwald, A.G. (1997). Validity concerns and usefulness of student ratings of instruction. *American Psychologist* 52(11), 1182–86.

Haskell, R.E. (1997). Academic freedom, tenure, and student evaluation of faculty: galloping polls in the 21st Century. *Education Policy Analysis Archives*, 5(6), Available: *http://olam.ed.asu.edu/epaa/v5n6.html*

Haskell, R.E. (1998). Academic freedom, tenure, and student evaluation of faculty: galloping polls in the 21st Century. *ERIC/AE Digest.* Available: *http://www.ericdigest.org/1999-3/freedom.htm*

Hoyt, D.P. and Pallett, W.H. (1999). Appraising teaching effectiveness – beyond student ratings. *IDEA Paper no 36(36).*

Kulik, J.A. (2001). Student ratings – validity, utility and controversy. *New Directions for Institutional Research*, 109, 9–25.

Lewin, L.O., Singh, M., Bateman, B.L. & Glover, P.B. (2009). Improving education in primary care: development of an online curriculum using the blended learning model. *BMC Medical Education*, 9, 33.

Machell, D.F. (1989). A discourse on professional melancholia. *Community Review*, 9, 41–50.

Manipal Institute of Health Sciences, Manipal. Info available at: *www.manipal.edu*

Marsh, H.W. (1984). Students' evaluation of university teaching: dimensionality, reliability, validity, potential biases and utility. *J Educational Psychology*, 76, 707–754.

Marsh, H.W. (1987). Students' evaluations of university teaching: research findings, methodological issues and future directions. *International Journal of Educational Research*, 11, 253–388.

McKeachie, W.J. (1997). Student ratings: the validity of use. *American Psychologist*, 52(11), 1218–25.

Medical Council of India. List of colleges and courses. Available at: *www.mciindia.org/InformationDesk/CollegesCoursesSearch.aspx*

Miller, R.I. (1987). *Evaluating faculty for promotion and tenure.* San Francisco: Jossey Bass.

National Assessment and Accreditation Council. Available at: *www.naac.gov.in/assessment_accreditation.html*

Naftulin, D.H., Ware, J.E., and Donnelly, F.A. (1973). The Doctor Fox lecture: a paradigm of educational seduction. *J Medical Education*, 48(7), 630–635.

National Knowledge Commission (NKC). (2006). Report of the Working Group on Medical Education. Available at: *http://knowledgecommission.gov.in/reports/report06.asp*

OIRA (Office of institutional research & assessment, Syracuse University). Student ratings of teaching effectiveness: creating an action plan. Available at: *http://oira.syr.edu/oira/-private/pdf/Action.pdf.*

Ory, J.C., Braskamp, L.A. and Pieper, D.M. (1980). The congruency of student evaluative information collected by three methods. *Journal of Educational Psychology,* 72, 181–185.

Overall, J.U., Marsh, H.W. (1980). Students' evaluations of instructions – a longitudinal study of their stability. *Journal of Educational Psychology,* 72, 321–325.

Purkiss, J., et al. (2012). Improving curriculum evaluation by expanding medical student participation: early successes with a multifaceted approach: *University of Michigan Medical School* RIME 2012 abstract.

Seldin, P. (1984). *Changing Practices in Faculty Evaluation.* San Francisco: Jossey-Bass.

Seldin, P. (1993). The use and abuse of student ratings of professors. *Chronicle of Higher Education,* 39, 40–45.

Seldin, P. (1997). Using student feedback to improve teaching. *To Improve the Academy* : Higher Education Administration Commons, Paper 393.

Seldin, P. (1999). Current practices – good and bad – nationally. In: Seldin, P. and Associates (Ed.) *Changing Practices in Evaluating Teaching,* pp 1–24. Bolton, MA: Anker Publishing Co.

Shankar, P.R, Piryani, R.M., Singh, K.K. et al (2012). Student feedback about the use of role plays in Sparshanam, a medical humanities module. Available at: *http:////f1000r.es/SWKxOt).*

Singh, T., Singh, D., Natu, M.V. and Zachariah, A. (1991). Hawthorne effect – a tool for improving the quality of medical education. *Indian J of Medical Education,* 30, 33–37.

Singh, T., Modi, J.N. (2012). The Quarter Model: A proposed approach to in-training assessment for undergraduate students in Indian Medical Schools. *Indian Pediatrics,* 49: 871–78.

Sixbury, G.R., Cashin, W.E. (1995). Description of database for the IDEA diagnostic form. *IDEA Technical report no 9.*

Stone, J.E. (1995). Inflated grades, inflated enrolment, and inflated budgets: an analysis and call for review at the state level. *Educational Policy Review Analysis Archives,* 3, No. 11(2075). (Online) Available: *http://olam.edu./epaa/v3n11.html*

Sood, R. & Adkoli, B.V. (2000). Medical education in India – problems and prospects (editorial) *Journal of Indian Academy of Clinical Medicine, 1 (3), 210–212.*

Sood, R. (2008). Medical education in India. *Medical Teacher, 30 (6),* 585–591.

Theall, M. and Franklin, J.L. (2001). Looking for bias in all the wrong places. *New Directions for Institutional Research,* 109, 45–56.

Theall, M. and Franklin, J.L. (1991). Using student ratings for teaching improvements. In Theall M. and Franklin J.L. (Eds) *New Directions for teaching and learning,* 48, 83–96.

Theall, M. (1996). When meta analysis is not enough. *Instructional evaluation and faculty development,* 15, 1–14.

Ware, J.E. & Williams, R.J. (1975). The Dr Fox effect: A study of lecturer effectiveness and ratings of instruction. *Journal of Medical Education*, 50(2), 149–56.

Wilson, R. (1998). New research casts doubt on value of student evaluation of professors. *The Chronicle of Higher Education*, pp A12–14.

Wines, W.A. & Lan, T.J. (2006). Observations on the folly of using student evaluations of college teaching for faculty evaluation, pay, and retention decisions and its implications for academic freedom, *William & Mary Journal of Women & law*. 167. Available: *http://scholarship.law.wm.edu/wmjowl/vol13/iss1/4*.

Young, R.D. (1993). Student evaluation of faculty: a faculty perspective. *Perspective on Political Science*, 22, 12–16.

Clerks' and Residents' Contributions to Building a Safe Educational Environment in a Medical Teaching Hospital: the Role of a System of Educational Quality Management (SEQM)

Monica van de Ridder,
Albert Schweitzer Hospital (ASz), the Netherlands

Abstract: A safe educational environment is crucial for learning. It influences patient safety and motivation of trainees and supervisors, creates learning opportunities, and it also improves performance. A learning environment can be kept safe when trainees and staff reinforce the good aspects in work-based teaching and learning practice and recognise, acknowledge, and report the aspects that can be improved. A System of Educational Quality Management (SEQM) used in a Dutch tertiary medical teaching hospital will be described in this chapter. Characteristics of the SEQM are the participation of clerks, residents, and staff, its focus on the learning environment, supervisors' teaching qualities, and the Plan-Do-Check-Act (PDCA) cycle. Outcomes are transparently communicated to the hospital board, programme directors, learners, and other hospitals. This chapter focusses on the question of how clerks and residents can contribute to enhancing a safe educational learning environment in a teaching hospital: what they do and how they are facilitated.

Keywords: Baseline measure; exit interviews; feedback system; internal audit; learning environment, Plan-Do-Check-Act-cycle; residents' evaluation; students' evaluation; teaching

Abbreviations

B-PDC – Board of Programme Directors Committee

CanMEDS – Canadian Medical Education Directions for Specialists

CBOG – College voorBeroepen en Opleidingen in de Gezondheidszorg

DOPS – Direct Observation of Procedural Skills

D-RECT – Dutch Residents Educational Climate Test

GME – Graduate Medical Education

KNMG – Royal Dutch Medical Association

Mini-CEX – Mini Clinical Evaluation Exercise

OSATS – Objective Structured Assessment of Technical Skills

PDCA-cycle – Plan-Do-Check-Act-cycle

PDC – Programme Directors Committee

PME – Postgraduate Medical Education

PHEEM – Postgraduate Hospital Educational Environment Measure

RA – Residents' Association

RTP – Residents' Training Programme

SEQM – System of Educational Quality Management

SETQ – System for Evaluation of Teaching Qualities

STZ – Association of Medical Teaching Hospitals

SWOT-analyses – Strengths Weakness Opportunities and Threats Analyses

WFME – World Federation of Medical Education

Introduction

Within higher education contexts around the world, it is now relatively common for students to evaluate their teachers (e.g. Richardson, 2005; Clayson, 2009; Spooren, Brockx, & Mortelmans, 2013). When a course is finished, data is collected, and the outcomes are shared with teachers, policymakers, and the institution. The information is used for improving teaching quality, providing input for tenure and promotion decisions, and for demonstrating the presence of adequate procedures for ensuring teaching quality (Kember, Leung, & Kwan, 2002).

This chapter describes how this evaluation process takes place in a workplace learning context in medical education in the Netherlands.

Medical students (clerks), who are enrolled in clerkship programmes but are also residents in training to become medical specialists participate in evaluations. The focus of the evaluations is: a) the organisation, quality of education, and facilities in the residents' and clerks' training programmes; b) the learning environment within training programmes, and c) the teaching qualities of the supervisors.

The importance of a safe learning environment will be illustrated in a fictitious example about Marian, a resident in training in a dermatology department. Further, it will be explained how a feedback system (an example of monitoring of education quality within the Dutch context) influences the learning environment. This will be made explicit by describing how clerks and residents contribute to the System of Educational Quality Management (SEQM), which is used for this purpose. The chapter closes by outlining the strengths, weakness, opportunities, and threats to the evaluation procedure and some concluding remarks.

Marian's story

Marian is in her second year of residency training. She likes patient contact, to puzzle over clinical cases, being on wards, and supervising the young clerks. In the dermatology department, the atmosphere among the residents in training is very good: they help each other, and the seniors make sure the junior residents feel accepted and comfortable. When it is busy, they take over each other's duties if necessary. The residents are backing up each other and they are a team.

On the other hand, she knows that there are conflicts among the medical specialists, and there is a lack of unity among them. Sometimes, her supervisors talk negatively about each other, and recently, one asked for her opinion on a personal conflict between colleagues. Marian feels uncomfortable, because she does not want to take sides. Since this happened, she avoids working with this supervisor.

Personal issues among the specialists create tensions and a negative atmosphere within the department. As a consequence, the residents in training do not feel safe and hesitate to ask for feedback. Marian notices that she hesitates to discuss dilemmas she faces with her supervisors: 'When they talk negatively about each other, it means that they also criticise residents'. Further, she notices that she has started hesitating to ask for feedback. And when she receives unsolicited feedback, from one of the medical specialists, she perceives it as unprofessional.

The situation has been discussed among the other dermatology residents and many of them are looking forward to going to another hospital, despite the nice fellow-residents and the camaraderie among them.

Determinants of the learning environment

A safe learning environment is an important precondition of workplace learning for both medical clerks and residents: '...[it] should facilitate learning behavior in work teams because it alleviates excessive concern about others' reactions to actions that have the potential for embarrassment or threat, which learning behaviors often have.' (Edmondson, 1999, 355). Research shows that a safe learning environment affects perceptions, motivation, satisfaction, and performance (Pritchard & Karasick, 1973; DeCotiis & Summers, 1987; Boor, 2009). Especially in the hospital setting, a safe learning environment is important, because clerks and residents are involved in patient care. Being afraid to ask supervisors for an opinion, or doubting the credibility of feedback, can affect patient care.

Baars-van Moorsel (2004) defines a learning environment as the conditions for the optimal functioning of learners. Examples of these conditions are the structure and culture within an organisation, the relationship between people, how well learners are prepared for transitions, and whether feedback is given.

Structure is an important determinant of the learning environment (Ende, Pozen, & Levinsky, 1986; Van der Hem-Stokroos, Daelmans, Scherpbier, van der Vleuten, de Vries, & Haarman, 2001; Remmen, Denekens, Scherpbier, Van der Vleuten, Hermann, Puymbroeck, & Bossaert, 1998; Bloom & Sheerer, 1992; Govaerts, Van der Vleuten, Schuwirt, & Muijtens, 2006; Durak, Vatansever, Van Dalen, & Van der Vleuten, 2007). Characteristics of structure are the organisation of an institute and the clarity of its procedures. In general, when learners feel there is a structure in which education and learning experiences are organised, they learn more and they feel more at ease.

Culture, such as the values and norms within an organisation, is also important (Jones, 2007; Baars-van Moorsel, 2004). It determines the general well-being of learners and employees (Baars-van Moorsel, 2004; Barbara & Pettitt, 2005; Boor, 2009; Joe et al, 2007; Van Hell, Kuks, & Cohen-Schotanus, 2009, Van der Hem-Stokroos, 2005).

Feedback is specific information about a comparison between an observation and a standard, given with the intent to improve learners' performance (van de Ridder et al, 2008). The way feedback is given affects learners' well-being and performance (Van Hell et al, 2009; Van der Hem-Stokroos, 2005; Boor, 2009; Daelmans, Van der Hem-Stokroos, Scherpbier, Stehouwer, & Van der Vleuten, 2006; Govaerts, van der Vleuten, Schuwirth, & Muijtjens, 2006; Remmen et al, 1998). When feedback influences performance, this does not always mean that performances automatically improve (e.g. Ilgen, Fisher, & Taylor, 1979; Kluger & DeNisi, 1996; Veloski, Boex, Grasberger, Evans, & Wolfson, 2006).

The learning environment is also determined by the *quality of relations* that learners and co-workers have with each other. When clerks and residents feel a part of a team, or feel welcome in the new environment and are welcomed by their supervisors, this has a positive effect on their learning (Boor, 2009; Lange & Baillie, 2008; Boor et al, 2008; Busari, 2004; Van der Hem-Stokroos, 2005; Van Hell et al, 2009; Booi, 2007; Van der Hem-Stokroos, 2005).

Feedback system

The case of Marian illustrates that a safe learning environment cannot be taken for granted. In her case, relations between residents were good, but the relationship between residents and supervisors lacked confidentiality. As a consequence, the learners did not ask for feedback, they did not trust feedback when they received it, and they were afraid to discuss difficult situations with their supervisors. If the learning environment was regularly evaluated, these difficulties probably would have been identified and discussed. According to the author's own observation, this creates opportunities for stakeholders, such as the medical specialists within the department, the residents and the clerks, to work actively on improving the learning environment.

To monitor processes, such as the learning environment, four steps need to be taken (Anderson, Rungtusanatham, & Schroeder, 1994; Kanji, 1996). In the *plan-phase,* objectives are formulated to further improve the learning environment in areas that are identified as being weak, and goals are also set to maintain good practices. In the *do-phase,* these goals are made specific and participants contribute to the achievement of the goals. The learning environment is measured in the *check-phase*, to determine whether or not the goals have reduced the gap between actual practice and preferred practice. In the *act-phase,* outcomes are compared with the past, and it is determined whether goals have been reached. If necessary, adjustments will be made. Based on this information, practice might be adjusted, and new goals may be set in the next *plan-phase.*

This four-phase process is known as the Deming-cycle or Plan-Do-Check-Act (PDCA) cycle (Anderson, Rungtusanatham, & Schroeder,

1994; Kanji, 1996). The PDCA-cycle is a model which is used in many quality management systems both within business organisations (Anderson et al, 1996; Carder & Ragan, 2003; Kanji, 1996) but also in higher education, as Owlia and Aspinwall (1997) describe it in their review. When a PDCA-cycle is used, this results in a *constant* monitoring of the quality of the learning environment. The information from learning environment measures serves as *input*, which then leads to actions to improve the system, the *output*. These actions influence the learning environment and result in new information. A circular process in which output is fed back as new input to modify the output of a system. In the given example (Marian's case), the learning environment is a *feedback system* (Encyclopaedia Britannica, 1992; Van de Ridder et al, 2008; Murray, 2012).

The central question in this chapter is: how can learners, be they clerks or residents, contribute to a safe learning environment by participating in a feedback system? To answer this question, a feedback system which is used in a Dutch teaching hospital will be described. Secondly, the role and the contribution of clerks and residents will be explained. The chapter will close with an evaluation of strengths, weaknesses, opportunities, and threats in the feedback system and the learners' participation in the SEQM.

Description of a System of Educational Quality Management (SEQM)

History

In 2002, the *Royal Dutch Medical Association* (KNMG) produced a report highlighting the necessity of changing postgraduate medical education (PME). This conclusion was due to changes in Dutch society, such as aging and increase in chronic diseases, and changes in the healthcare system, for example the transition from supply-oriented towards demand-oriented care, the rapid development of scientific knowledge and technology, the increase in female physicians, and a demand for regular working hours in which family and work could be combined. According to the report, PME did not fit the needs of the future, and clerks and residents were not prepared for tomorrow's care (CBOG, 2008; KNMG, 2002; Ten Cate, Bleker, Büller, & Scherpbier, 2003).

The impact of this report on PME was significant. In graduate medical education (GME), curricula had been reformed regularly. This was not the case in PME. In the Netherlands, the Canadian Medical Education Directions for Specialists (CanMEDS) was adopted, and based on the CanMEDS final attainment levels, the outcomes were formulated and information-rich activities were identified (Frank & Danoff, 2007; Scheele et al, 2008). Assessment and reflection tools such as the Mini-Clinical Evaluation Exercise (Mini-CEX), Direct Observation of Procedural Skills (DOPS), and Objective Structured Assessment of Technical Skills (OSATS), were used to assess the learner, to foster reflection, and to provide feedback (Norcini & Burch, 2007; Scheele et al, 2008; Miller & Archer, 2010). Many medical staff members are acquainted with these tools and use them frequently. It becomes clear to learners and staff that these tools provide valuable information on clerks' and residents' progress. Monitoring the progress of residents' professional development became more transparent. With this information, it has become easier for residents to set learning goals and to ask for specific feedback.

A safe learning environment is an important precondition for the effectiveness of workplace-based assessment and feedback (Hewson & Little, 1998). This is also illustrated in the case of Marian when she hesitates to ask for feedback. When feedback is a threat to self-esteem, its effectiveness is low (Kluger & DeNisi, 1996). Additionally, when it is given in public, it is disliked (Hewson & Little, 1998).

This need for a safe learning environment has been widely acknowledged. In the Netherlands, the *College voor de Beroepen en Opleidingen in de Gezondheidszorg* (CBOG) was an advisory body of the Dutch government on medical and healthcare professions and education between 2006 and 2012. The CBOG (2008) developed quality indicators based on the accreditation standards of the *World Federation of Medical Education* (WFME) (2003) to stimulate internal quality assurance of education. The quality indicators are based on four domains:

a) Regional education – this is the responsibility of the collaborating teaching hospitals and the university medical centres.

b) Educational facilities and requirements for hospitals – this is the responsibility of the hospital board and board of programme directors.

c) Educational facilities and requirements for medical staff and learners at the departmental level – this is the responsibility of each programme director and medical staff within a department.

d) Quality of residents' education, and the activities they are involved in – this is also the responsibility of each programme director, the medical staff, and residents within a department.

The *Association of Tertiary Medical Teaching Hospitals* (STZ) also introduced quality indicators regarding education, research, and top clinical care (STZ, 2011). Many of STZ's educational quality indicators underline the fact that monitoring of educational quality needs to be done at a departmental and hospital level.[1] The quality indicators for medical education formed two systems that overlapped. Using different sets of quality indicators for monitoring educational quality did not seem practical. Therefore, the B-PDC developed a system in which the quality indicators were brought together.

The development of a System for Educational Quality Management

From 2009 to 2013, a System for Educational Quality Management (SEQM) was developed, in which the quality criteria of both STZ and CBOG served as a starting point. The SEQM was based upon instruments which were already in use. A clerkship evaluation questionnaire had been used since 2007, the Dutch Residency Educational Climate Test (D-RECT) since 2008, and surgeons had been using the System of Evaluation of Teaching Qualities (SETQ) since 2009. In 2010, the SETQ came into use in all teaching departments, and internal audits and pre-visits for accreditation were also introduced. In 2011, baseline measures were added and, in 2012-2013, the procedure for exit interviews was developed. Each instrument in which learners participate will be described in the next section.

The Programme Directors Committee (PDC), the hospital board, and the Residents Association (RA) approved the SEQM and mandated the Board of Programme Directors Committee (B-PDC) to monitor the educational environment. In practice, this means the B-DPC invites the assessors and prepares the sessions when baseline measures, exit interviews, internal audits and pre-visits for accreditation are performed. The assessors discuss the outcomes from all instruments with the different stakeholders (Table 6.2) and monitor the actions following from the outcomes. They also plan a follow-up and work closely together with members of the PDC, the RA, and if necessary also with the Human Resource Department (HRD) (see Table 6.1).

Table 6.1 Description of the instruments used in the SEQM of the Albert Schweitzer Hospital

Instrument	Focus	Participants	Frequency	Duration minutes	Assessors SEQM			
					B-PDC	RA	PDC	HRD
Clerkship evaluation	Organisation, education, facilities, and learning environment of training programme	Clerks	Upon leaving clerk	15	Internal electronic system			
Baseline measure	Organisation, education, facilities of RTP	Residents and programme deputy directors	Biennial	120	■			
Pre-visit for accreditation	Organisation, education, facilities, and learning environment of RTP	Residents and supervisors	Before accreditation	120	■	■	■	
Internal audit	Organisation, education, facilities, and learning environment of RTP	Residents	Biennial	90	■	■	■	
D-RECT	Learning environment	Residents	Annual	15	External electronic system			
SETQ	Individual teaching qualities of supervisors	Residents and supervisors	Annual	R: 20-90 S: 20	External electronic system			
Exit interviews	Organisation, education, facilities, and learning environment of RTP	Residents	Upon leaving resident	60	■	■		■

B-PDC) Board of Programme Director Committee, RA) Residents' Association, PDC) Programme Directors Committee, HRD) Human Resource Development, S) supervisors, R) residents.

Table 6.2

Table 6.2 Overview of the outcome level and stakeholders with whom the reports are shared

Instrument	Outcome level:	Presentation of information	Stakeholders with who reports can be shared					
			Department	B-PDC	PDC	RA	Hospital Board	Others
Clerkship evaluation	Department	Quantitative and open comments	■	■	■	■	■	
Baseline measure	Department	Quantitative and open comments	■	■				
Pre-visit for accreditation	Department	Narrative	■	■				
Internal audit	Department	Narrative	■	■	■	■	■	
D-RECT	Department	Quantitative and open comments	■	■	■	■	■	
	Hospital	Quantitative	■	■	■	■	■	■
SETQ	Individual	Quantitative and open comments						
	Department	Quantitative	■	■	■	■	■	
	Hospital	Quantitative	■	■	■	■	■	■
Exit interviews	Department/ individual	Narrative		■				

B-PDC) Board of Programme Director Committee, PDC) Programme Directors Committee, and RA) Residents' Association

The goal of the SEQM is to increase patient safety, improve patient care, and provide a safe learning environment for both medical staff and learners by: 1) establishing a culture within the hospital of monitoring the learning environment by going through a PDCA-cycle, and 2) stimulating the development and use of a PDCA-cycle at a departmental level through the active participation of medical staff and learners in the SEQM.

The programme directors of each medical specialty are charged with implementing the PDCA-cycle. They have to write an annual report in which action points are that will be carried out in the year ahead are delineated. They also have to write an annual evaluation in which they describe their goals and evaluate the effects of their actions.

Instruments used in the SEQM

The SEQM consists of seven different instruments (Table 6.1) in which learners are involved. Other instruments are also used, such as administrative lists of medical staff who are involved in teach-the-teacher programmes[2], or who participate in assessments for personal development, etc. The seven instruments cover three different themes: a) the organisation, quality of education, and facilities of the residents' and clerks' training programme; b) the learning environment within the training programme, and c) the teaching qualities of the supervisors. Due to the focus of this chapter, only instruments in which learners are involved will be described. What do these instruments measure and how is a follow-up organised?

Clerkship Evaluation

The clerkship evaluation questionnaire is used to measure the learning environment in clerkships of the different departments in the hospital. Since 2007, a translated version of the Postgraduate Hospital Education Environment Measurement (PHEEM) is used. This questionnaire was developed by Roff, McAleer, and Skinner (2005) to evaluate the learning environment in residency training programmes in the United Kingdom. While the PHEEM is widely used internationally, its validity is disputed (Boor, Scheele, Van der Vleuten, Scherpbier, Teunissen, & Sijtsma, 2007; Clapham, Wall, & Batchelor, 2007; Schönrock-Adema, Heijne-Penninga, Van Hell, & Cohen-Schotanus, 2009). Therefore the scales proposed by

Roff (2005) are not used, but the items are used as indicators to highlight good aspects and aspects for improvement, and as a guide to stimulate discussion of the quality of the clerkship environment. Some specific questions tailored to the Albert Schweitzer Hospital setting have been added. The questions are answered on a five-point Likert scale (1 = not at all important – 5 = highly important). Based on a qualitative study by Wijnia (2010), open-ended questions have also been added. Clerks sometimes perceive learning experiences as negative (for example, when they receive too much responsibility). It is important to recognise what these experiences are and why they are perceived as negative. When information on negative learning experiences is not explicitly explored, clerks' negative learning experiences will be undetected, and no actions will be taken to prevent this from happening. To know which learning experiences could be stimulated, clerks are also asked to report on their positive learning experiences.

The clerkship evaluation questionnaire is filled out in the last week of each clerkship. It takes approximately 15 minutes. The hardest aspect is to monitor that all clerks actually do complete the questionnaire. Sometimes clerkship directors forget to ask and this can undermine the reliability of the questionnaire at a departmental level.

A report of the qualitative and quantitative results at a departmental level is given back to the clerkship programme directors. When item scores are lower than 3.5, it is agreed that an item needs to be improved. Clerkship directors are asked to discuss the report with the residents and medical staff within the department, and to report on actions for improvement.

Baseline Measure

The baseline measure is a questionnaire tailored to the Dutch context and consists of a set of quality indicators (CBOG, 2008). These quality indicators are based on the accreditation standards for PME as formulated by the WFME (2003). The baseline measure has incorporated indicators that refer to the domain of the department. 14 questions capture medical staff development regarding education, and 9 items are about the content and organisation of the Residency Training Programme (RTP) for each department. The residents' 16 items are focussed on the activities residents perform during their training, such as their involvement in research, and how the group of residents is functioning. The answers have to be filled out on a five-point scale. A low score indicates a low integration of the topic in the PDCA-cycle, while a high score indicates that the PDCA-cycle functions well. The baseline measure is discussed in a small group, consisting of the programme director, programme deputy director, and two residents. The discussion is moderated by an external person, generally a member of the B-PDC. When the score for each question has been determined, the group must propose what needs to be done to reach a higher score. This is all then recorded, and it results in an action plan. The more specific the notes on how to improve are, the more they can be used as guidelines for medical staff and residents to further develop the organisation, education, and facilities of the RTP. The outcomes of the baseline measure can be shared with other residents and medical staff within the department. The baseline measure is carried out every two years, and this takes about 120 minutes.

Pre-visit for accreditation

In the Netherlands, only accredited bachelor's and master's degree programmes receive government funding (Brouwer, 2004). Therefore, once every six years, the clerkship programmes are audited for accreditation. Further, only accredited residency training programmes are allowed to educate residents. Residency training programmes are visited every two to five years, and accreditation criteria are in line with the guidelines of the WFME (2003).

A pre-visit for accreditation is an internal visit which generally takes place between two and six months before the real accreditation visit is scheduled. The goal of the pre-visit for accreditation is to show the residents, clerks and medical staff what will happen during the accreditation visit. It also checks whether gaps crucial for the accreditation visit can be identified. Three members of the B-PDC, one member of the PDC who recently experienced an accreditation visit, and a member of the RA visit a department and follow the procedures which are used when the accreditation committee is visiting the department. The panel asks questions that are also expected to be asked during the accreditation visit. When the panel, for example, notices that the learner's personal development plan is not filled out in the portfolio, or that medical staff do not give feedback with the Mini-CEX, this is reported back to the staff and programme directors. Small things can be improved before the actual accreditation visit takes place.

The pre-visit for accreditation takes about two hours. First, members of the panel speak with all the students and residents in the department. Then, they speak with all the staff about the organisation of the education, the facilities, and organisation of the supervision. They also check whether requirements and suggestions from the last accreditation have been fulfilled. At the conclusion of the pre-visit, they report all their findings back to students, residents, staff and programme directors. The member of the RA then prepares a short report in which the points for improvement are summarised.

Internal Audit

Internal audits are commonly used in medical education. According to Ivers et al (2012), the effect of an audit and the information that is fed back can have a small but important impact on daily practice. The goal of an internal audit is to solicit more specific and detailed information about the learning environment compared with the information generated by the D-RECT, SETQ, or clerkship evaluation. With this instrument, problems related to a safe learning environment can be detected at an early stage.

The internal audit consists of an in-depth discussion between two members of the B-PDC, a PDC member who has been recently audited, and a member of the RA, with the residents from another department. In general, the audit takes 90 minutes and the discussion follows a structured format along relevant themes, such as: the quality of the daily supervision; the scientific supervision; facilities for personal development, and structure of feedback and assessment. The member of the RA then writes a report. An internal audit takes place every two years, and it alternates with the baseline measure. In some instances, another internal audit can be carried out. This happens when the B-PDC receives signals that learners perceive the learning environment as unsafe, when a group of residents does not want to fill out the SETQ because they are afraid that the results will be used against them, or based on information from exit interviews.

The residents prepare a report from the meeting and this is first sent to the internal audit panel. When they have edited the report, it is sent to the residents in the department. They edit the report in such a way that they feel comfortable with it. Then the final report is sent to the programme director and deputy director. They are asked to discuss it with the staff, and then the internal audit panel discuss the report with the staff and ask them to act upon the points for improvement. Then, an action plan is prepared. The report is discussed in the PDC, so that all programme directors can learn from it.

When serious issues are identified, a different procedure is adopted. The internal audit panel presents and discusses the report only with the programme director and deputy director, then the panel visits the whole group to discuss the programme and request an action plan. The report and the action plan will not be discussed in the PDC. Six months later, a second audit takes place and the report and action plan are discussed in the PDC, and with other stakeholders as well. The internal audit procedure is important to guarantee confidentiality and safety for both residents and staff. A negative report can be perceived as a threat to the department and influence group dynamics. Therefore it is important to highlight that it is a tool everybody can learn from.

Dutch Residency Educational Climate Test (D-RECT)

The D-RECT was developed in 2008 by Boor and colleagues (Boor, 2011). As mentioned earlier, the validity and reliability of some of the learning environment tests has been disputed (Boor et al, 2007; Schönrock-Adema et al, 2009). Therefore an instrument for the Dutch context was developed. The purpose of the D-RECT is to gain insight into residents' perceptions of the learning environment in a hospital department, an outpatient clinic, or on the wards. The D-RECT consists of 50 items which are answered on a five-point scale (1 = not relevant – 5 = highly relevant). This results in 11 sub-scales, such as: supervision, teamwork, feedback, peer collaboration, and professional relations among physicians. There is also a space for comments.

An external party produces reports at a departmental level. Based on the outcomes of the departmental reports, a hospital report can be prepared. The B-PDC asks the programme directors to discuss the findings with the medical staff, residents, and students. In small departments with a lack of anonymity, it is not clear how reliably the D-RECT is filled out. When residents within small departments feel safe, they generally fill out the questionnaire. The D-RECT is filled out annually and this takes about 15 minutes.

Teaching Evaluation System (SETQ)

The aim of the SETQ is to measure the quality of supervisors' teaching and aims to improve teaching through feedback (Van der Leeuw, Lombarts, Heineman, & Arah, 2011). The electronic SETQ questionnaire (22 items) consists of five scales: learning environment, professional attitude and treatment of residents, communication of goals, staff evaluation of residents, and feedback (Lombarts, Arah, Busch, & Heineman, 2010; Van der Leeuw et al, 2011).

Medical staff evaluate their own teaching skills, and residents fill out the questionnaire assessing staff members with whom they collaborate. The most important section is the part in which residents write down suggestions and open comments.

Each supervisor receives a personal report in which their self-evaluation is compared with the residents' evaluation. Besides the personal report, the staff also receive a report within a department, which gives an indication of their teaching quality within the department. The outcomes of both reports should be discussed with both staff and residents in a safe environment, to determine what can be improved. The degree of openness within departments varies, therefore some programme directors ask an external person to mediate this discussion and also help staff with formulating explicit points for improvement. The SETQ is filled out annually and it takes about 15 minutes for staff and up to 90 minutes for residents, depending on how many staff they evaluate.

Exit interviews

The exit interviews are widely used as a quality improvement instrument in healthcare, especially to explore the reasons why people leave an organisation (McConnel, 1992; Webster, Flint, & Courtney, 2009; Flint & Webster, 2013). This tool is often used in nursing practice, but information on the use of exit interviews in medical education is scarce. Interviews with representatives of the 28 medical teaching hospitals have shown that they are either using exit interviews or considering using them. When only a few residents are working in a department (n<5), the D-RECT and SETQ can give biased information, because learners do not feel comfortable filling in the questionnaire. To obtain more reliable information from this group, an exit interview can be useful. Information about the learning environment, the supervision and the learning facilities and opportunities can be discussed. When a clerk or resident leaves, they typically have a meeting with the programme director to reflect on their clerkship or residency. The programme director evaluates the residents and clerks, so they depend on the programme director for a reference. This dependency can also lead to biased information about points for improvement. Therefore, the exit interview with the resident is held by a member of the B-PDC, or a HRD employee and a member of the RA. Those who hold the exit interview are from a different discipline than the learner.

All residents receive a short online questionnaire six weeks before they leave the hospital. This serves as preparation and input for the exit interview. Residents from small departments (<5 residents) all receive an invitation and residents from large groups only receive an invitation if they request an exit interview.

Once a year, a summary of anonymous information from the exit interviews is shared with the PDC. When students or residents report urgent information (for example, malpractice of supervisors, or situations that are a threat to clerks or residents) that requires immediate action, steps that will be taken are first discussed with the resident. Only by carefully handling sensitive information and protecting the residents as an information source can unnecessary damage be avoided.

If one of these seven instruments had been used in Marian's case, she and her colleagues would have had an opportunity to address the issues in their department. And the B–PDC probably would have taken some action.

How can residents contribute to the improvement of the system?

Roles of learners linked to the PDCA-cycle

Learners have four different roles in the whole feedback process. They are the key information providers on the learning environment. They provide information on the learning environment when filling out the D-RECT or the clerkship evaluation. They give insight on the teaching qualities of supervisors when it comes to the SETQ. During the internal audit, the pre-visit for accreditation or the baseline measure, learners also provide information on the organisation, including the quality and facilities of the education they receive in the hospital.

Members of the Resident's Association can also fulfill the role of assessors (Table 6.1). Together with the members of the Board of Programme Directors, they prepare internal audits, pre-visits for accreditation, and exit interviews, and they participate in assessing staff and learners from a specific department. They ask questions, and often write a report on the findings. When outcomes are fed back to the stakeholders, they also participate in this process. It is highly valuable when a learner participates as an assessor. They understand other learners and they know, often from informal contact with residents and clerks, which items are important. Residents and medical staff are never assessors in their own departments.

Table 6.2 shows that results are discussed with staff, residents, and other learners. They discuss the consequences of the outcomes, identify needs, and try to find solutions together with the medical staff on how to meet their needs. They also identify new goals, and are considered critical partners.

The roles of learners can be easily linked to the different phases in the PDCA-cycle (Figure 6.1). In the check-phase, in which the quality of the learning environment needs to be systematically measured, residents and students provide information and some of them will also fulfill the role of assessors. In the act-phase, learners think about changes that would

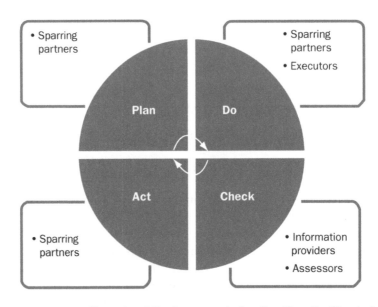

Figure 6.1 The role of the learners during the Plan-Do-Check-Act cycle in the SEQM

improve the quality of learning, and they help identify the gap between actual and preferred practice. They are critical partners here too. This is also their role when new goals are set in the plan-phase, and are carried out in the do-phase. In the do-phase, learners also contribute to the achievement of new goals.

Stimulation of participation

Residents and clerks are active participants in the quality improvement of their own training programme. For them to participate, it's key for them to feel comfortable. This means that learners have to know that the information they provide about the learning environment, the teaching qualities of their supervisors, the organisation, and the facilities of the training programme are treated confidentially. Programme directors play an important role in giving this guarantee and also in instructing staff how to deal with information which they think comes from a certain clerk or resident. When procedures around information sharing and discussion are clear, this increases stakeholders' feeling of safety. Further, when a resident participates as an assessor, this is never in his/her own specialty. So, a psychiatry resident will be an assessor at an internal audit of neurology or clinical chemistry, but not in a pre-visit for accreditation of psychiatry.

When residents participate as assessors together with PDC members, they receive a Mini-CEX on the competence of scholars and professionalism, and subsequently receive feedback on their input.

The fact that members of the Residents' Association participate in the SEQM makes them good partners to discuss hospital education policy with. They are regularly invited to meetings with the PDC and hospital board to discuss changes and new ideas. Their input is highly valued. For example, programme directors felt that participating in the SETQ and D-RECT was too much of a burden for the residents, so they proposed to administer these questionnaires biannually. However, residents found it important to evaluate the learning environment and the qualities of teachers each year, because they considered it an important way to channel their ideas and voices. This is the main reason why these questionnaires are administered annually.

Strengths, weaknesses, opportunities, and threats of the SEQM and learners' participation

The Strengths, Weaknesses, Opportunities and Threats (SWOT) is an analytical tool that gives insight into the factors that are helpful and harmful to an organisation, a process, or a product. It analyses the internal and external factors of the environment or culture in which the organisation, product, or process functions. This results in a matrix in which the strengths, weaknesses, opportunities, and threats are presented (Helms & Nixon, 2010; Ghazinoory, Abdi, & Azadegan-Mehr, 2011). The SWOT-analysis was used for an intermittent evaluation of the present state of the SEQM, and the B-PDC identified the following strengths, weaknesses, opportunities and threats (as indicated below).

Strengths

The SETQ, D-RECT, and clerkship evaluation give some indication based on a numeric scale of learners' perceptions of the teaching qualities of their supervisors and the learning environments in their departments. The quantitative information does not express learners' in-depth perceptions. The comments provided in the baseline measures, the narrative reports from the pre-visits for accreditation, the internal audits and the exit interviews are highly valuable in helping to understand and interpret the data from the SETQ, D-RECT, and clerkship evaluation.

The narrative reports are carefully constructed, and the content is checked by the assessors, the residents, and/or the supervisors who were involved. This makes the information particularly valuable, and also reliable. The information can be easily accessed, checked, and looked up. The information from all these instruments together gives the B-PDC and other stakeholders a clear understanding of what the main points for improvement are, and also where improvement is required. Residents explained that when there were difficulties in the department or when the group of residents was small, they gave positive feedback in both the D-RECT and the SETQ to avoid 'fuss'. They indicated that they were sometimes afraid that negative feedback would have an adverse impact upon them.

By being clear about confidentiality and by facilitating a safe environment, learners tend to give honest answers, meaning the results of the questionnaires can be considered trustworthy. This trustworthiness

Table 6.3 Strengths, Weakness, Opportunities and Threats analysis of the SEQM

	Helpful	Harmful
Internal	Strengths • Valuable information is written down; • Points for improvement become clear; • It becomes visible what is really going on; • Close moderation of the quality process.	Weakness • Lack of motivation; • Time consuming; • Workload for residents and staff; • Poor organisation of follow-up; • Poor guarantee of confidentiality for residents and staff.
External	Opportunities • Makes the process transparent; • Proves what the learning environment is worth; • Residents learn about scholar, communication and professionalism roles (CanMEDS).	Threats • Dependent on others if the SETQ D-RECT system does not work; • Questionnaires that do not fit a department; • Implementing new instruments too soon: first a routine is needed.

further stimulates the department to take action on the points for improvement.

A third important point is that the SEQM stimulates the B-PDC to closely monitor the whole structure. Throughout the year, the B-PDC receives information from internal audits, exit interviews, pre-visits for accreditation, and baseline measures. So the SEQM is a repetitive topic on the agenda of the B-PDC meetings. In this way, the B-PDC stays focussed on the interventions. Programme directors and departments learn from each other by following good practices and sharing solutions to common problems.

Weaknesses

The SEQM only works when clerks, residents and staff are motivated and willing to put time and energy into quality improvement. The B-PDC is sensitive to motivational issues in both residents and staff. It is acknowledged that the SEQM is time-consuming, especially for residents who work in large departments. Filling out the SETQ can take sometimes up to 120 minutes. A concern was expressed that this was too much of a time commitment for the residents. Therefore, the RA was surveyed and members were asked how they wanted to complete the SETQ and D-RECT. They expressed a wish to complete these annually, which has given them the opportunity to express their opinions.

The SEQM is also time-consuming for the supervisors. They need to discuss the results at staff meetings in their departments. Therefore, the SEQM is tailored to the different needs of the programme directors and the departments with residency and clerkship programmes. It is hoped that this will relieve the burden on the department.

When the SETQ and D-RECT are conducted annually, this means that the outcomes have to be discussed with the supervisors within the departments, with the residents, and with the B-PDC. This takes at least four months. By the time decisions on follow-up are taken and implemented, only half a year is left until the next round of SETQ and D-RECT evaluations. The B-PDC has to be alert in organising its follow-up. At times, a department has made an effort to improve the situation. If the B-PDC takes too little notice, this could be demotivating for the programme director. It is important that improvements and good practice are shared with colleagues from other departments. Sharing good practice in the department offers a learning opportunity for other departments. It is important that programme directors have a space to share success stories regarding education; this is motivating and it leads to acknowledgement.

The most important aspect is that the B-PDC guarantees confidentiality of the SEQM for supervisors, residents, and clerks. The different types of instruments, especially internal audit and exit interviews, sometimes reveal sensitive information. For example, residents may indicate that they perceive the learning environment as unsafe, that they feel tensions between departments, or that residents are afraid of some supervisors, which affects their own performance and well-being. For the B-PDC, this information is important, and can be a spur to further investigate whether it can be supported by what actually happens on the ground. Therefore, it is important to be transparent about procedures, such as how the assessment was conducted and, more importantly, how information will be shared. Only when confidentiality can be guaranteed can the factors that hinder both residents and supervisors in their learning at work truly be revealed.

For medical staff, it is also important that safety is guaranteed, otherwise their willingness to look into problems diminishes. This can be resolved through transparency – when clear procedures about documenting information and regular evaluation are in place.

Opportunities

Before the SEQM was used, the PDC regularly discussed the learning environment. These discussions were general, dominated by impressions of programme directors, and facts were missing. The SEQM is used because it leads to more in-depth discussions, often illustrated by examples. The outcomes of D-RECT and SETQ affirm some general ideas, such as that the residents liked the hospital and that they felt that the medical staff treated them as colleagues. After using the baseline measure, the pre-visit for accreditation and the internal audit, the points for improvement become clearer. The information gained through utilising these instruments together gives a clearer picture of what happens in a workplace. Instead of roughly judging the quality of training programmes, the tools help generate outlines of the good aspects and points for improvement.

The SEQM was developed to make the process of monitoring educational quality more transparent for accreditation procedures during external audits. Experiences with the SEQM have also been presented at conferences and other professional meetings. The exchange of ideas with academics about monitoring educational quality gives new ideas, which leads to the improvement of the SEQM.

The CBOG (2008) has recommended the involvement of residents in their own training, by setting their own goals and involving them in shaping the local curriculum. If residents are involved in monitoring educational quality, they are helping to shape the local curriculum. When a pre-visit for accreditation is planned, it has been established that RA members are part of the delegation of the PDC. The RA member takes notes, writes a report, and is involved in asking questions. Residents know the context well and they easily detect problems related to residency issues. The residents are also present when results are discussed with the department. By participating as assessors, residents learn a lot about the educational aspects of the roles of supervisors and educators in practice.

Threats

As can be seen in Table 6.1, an external company organises the questionnaires electronically and also produces the qualitative reports. Technical errors, such as log-in problems or the loss of data, occur regularly. This leads to motivational difficulties among staff and residents. The users are dependent on the company's service.

For some departments, the questions in the D-RECT do not exactly fit their educational context. In these case, supervisors and residents find it hard to make a transfer to their specific context. In the clinical physics department, patient contact is not regular, but they have a lot of contact with other healthcare workers and collaborate within a team. So, patient-related questions are not directly relevant to them. The medical psychology department employs a different approach to supervision compared with the other medical specialties. Thus, some questions on supervision do not make sense in the medical psychology department. Working with a questionnaire that is not relevant to the particular context can also be demotivating. The focus of the discussion is on usefulness and reliability, and both residents and clerks forget that the aim of the questionnaire is not only to evaluate the quality of training programmes, but also as a tool to discuss workplace education.

The SEQM has a short history, so changing the system or adding new instruments has to be carefully considered. It is important that residents and academics get used to the system, the instruments, and use of the outcomes. Only when the SEQM is totally implemented and accepted can further adjustments be made.

Concluding remarks

The situation in Marian's department would have been detected and discussed if a SEQM had been in use. The B-PDC probably would have picked up signals from the D-RECT, SETQ, an exit interview and/or an internal audit. A 'neutral' mediator could have discussed these problems with the residents and medical staff. The B-PDC would have invited medical staff and residents of this department to prepare a plan to solve these issues, and to restore the 'safety' of the learning environment for both staff and residents.

An educational learning environment in a hospital can only be 'safe' if clerks and residents collaborate with academics in keeping it transparent by being open, and by turning points for improvement into learning situations. Involving learners in a feedback system such as the SEQM helps them learn early in their career about the importance of a well-functioning quality system and how to improve it. This experience can then serve as a good foundation for helping to keep the learning environment healthy when these students become staff themselves.

Acknowledgements

I am grateful to the members of the Board of Programme Directors, Rob Oostenbroek and François Verheijen, and Ikrame Oulad Abdennabi – member of the RA, for their comments on this chapter.

References

Anderson, J.C., Rungtusanatham, M. and Schroeder, R.G., 1994. A theory of quality management underlying the Deming management method. *The Academy of Management Review*, 19(3), 472–509.
Association of Tertiary Medical Teaching Hospitals (STZ), 2011. *Toelatings – en hervisitatiecriteria STZ-lidmaatschap [Admission and reaccreditation criteria STZ-membership]*. Association of Tertiary Medical Teaching Hospitals (STZ) viewed 3 October 2013 from: *http://www.stz.nl/pagina/44-toelatings-en-visitatiecriteria.html*
Baars-van Moorsel, M., 2004. Leerklimaat in ziekenhuizen [Learning climate in hospitals]. *Onderwijs en gezondheidszorg*, 28, 159–163.

Barbara, J. & Pettitt, M.D., 2005. Medical student concerns and fears before their third-year surgical clerkship. *The American Journal of Surgery*, 189, 492–496.

Bloom, P.J. and Sheerer, M., 1992. Changing organizations by changing individuals: a model of leadership training. *The Urban Review*, 24, 263–286.

Booi, H.K., 1997. Style and quality in research supervision: the supervisor dependency factor. *Higher Education*, 34, 81–103.

Boor, K., Scheele, F., Van der Vleuten, C.P.M., Scherpbier, A.J.J.A., Teunissen, P.W. and Sijtsma, K., 2007. Psychometric properties of an instrument to measure the clinical learning environment. *Medical Education*, 41, 92–99.

Boor, K., Teunissen, P.W., Scherpbier, A.J.J.A., Van der Vleuten, C.P.M., Van de Lande, J. and Scheele, F., 2008. Residents' perceptions of the ideal clinical teacher – a qualitative study. *European Journal of Obstetrics and Gynaecology and Reproductive Biology*, 140, 152–157.

Boor, K., 2009, *The clinical learning climate*. PhD thesis. Rotterdam: Klarke Boor.

Boor, K., Van der Vleuten, C., Teunissen, P., Scherpbier, A. and Scheele F., 2011. Development and analysis of D-RECT, an instrument measuring residents' learning climate. *Medical Teacher*, 33, 820–827.

Brouwer, O., 2004. *Quality assurance, accreditation and legal education in Europe*. NVAO, viewed 7 October 2013, from: *http://www.nvao.net/page/ downloads/Speech_Brouwer_Quality_assurance_accreditation_accreditation_ and_legal_education_in_Europe_nov_2004.pdf*

Busari, J. O., 2004. *The medical resident as a teacher. Teaching and learning in the clinical workplace*. PhD thesis. Amsterdam: Uitgeverij, Buijten & Schipperheijn.

Carder, B. and Ragan, P.W., 2003. A survey-based system for safety measurement and improvement. *Journal of Safety Research*, 34, 157–165.

CBOG, 2008. *Eindrapportage Projectgroep Kwaliteitsindicatoren [Final report Project group Quality Indicators]*. CBOG, viewed 25 October 2013 from: http://www.oorzon.nl/files/3813/1529/6181/Eindrapportage_projectgroep_ Kwaliteitsindicatoren11.pdf

Clapham, M., Wall, D. and Batchelor, A., 2007. Educational environment in intensive care medicine – use of Postgraduate Hospital Educational Environment Measure (PHEEM). *Medical Teacher*, 29, e184–e191.

Clayson, D. E., 2009. Student evaluations of teaching: are they related to what students learn? A meta-analysis and review of the literature. *Journal of Marketing Education*, 31, 16–30.

Daelmans, H.E.M., Overmeer, R.M., Van der Hem-Stokroos, H.H., Scherpbier, A.J.J.A., Stehouwer, C.D.A. and Van der Vleuten, C.P.M., 2006. In-training assessment: qualitative study of effects on supervision and feedback in an undergraduate clinical rotation. *Medical Education*, 40, 51–58.

DeCotiis, T.A. and Summers, T.P., 1987. A path analysis of a model of the antecedents and consequences of organizational commitment. *Human Relations*, 40, 445–470.

Durak, H.I., Vatansever, K., Van Dalen, K. and Van der Vleuten, C., 2007. Factors determining students' global satisfaction with clerkships: an analysis of a two year students' ratings database. *Advances in Health Science Education*, 13, 495–502.

Edmondson, A., 1999. Psychological Safety and Learning Behavior in Work Teams. *Administrative Science Quarterly*, 44(2), 350–383.

Encyclopaedia Britannica, 1992, *The New Encyclopaedia Britannica*, 15th ed. Chicago: Encyclopaedia Britannica, 715.

Ende, J., Pozen, J.T. and Levinsky, N.G., 1986, Enhancing learning during a clinical clerkship: the value of a structured curriculum. *Journal of General Internal Medicine*, 1, 232–237.

Flint, A. and Webster, J., 2013. The use of the exit interview to reduce turnover amongst healthcare professionals. *Cochrane Database of Systematic Reviews*, 1, 1–29.

Frank, J.R. and Danoff D., 2007. The CanMEDS initiative: implementing an outcomes-based framework of physician competencies. *Medical Teacher*, 29(7), 624–627.

Ghazinoory, S., Abdi, M. and Azadegan-Mehr, M., 2011. Swot methodology: a state-of-the-art review for the past, a framework for the future, *Journal of Business Economics and Management*, 12(1), 24–48.

Govaerts, M.J.B., Van der Vleuten, C., Schuwirth, W.T. and Muijtjens, A.M.M., 2006. The use of observational diaries in in-training evaluation: student perceptions. *Advances in Health Science Education*,10, 171–188.

Helms, M.M. and Nixon J., 2010, Exploring SWOT analysis – where are we now? A review of academic research from the last decade. *Journal of Strategy and Management*, 3(3), 215–251.

Hewson, M.G. and Little M.L., 1998. Giving feedback in medical education. *Journal of General Internal Medicine*, 13(2), 111–116.

Ilgen, D.R., Fisher, C.D. and Taylor, M.S., 1979, Consequences of individual feedback on behavior in organizations. *Journal of Applied Psychology*, 64(4), 349–371.

Ivers, N., Jamtvedt, G., Flottorp, S., Young, J.M., Odgaard-Jensen, J., French, S.D., O'Brien, M.A., Johansen, M., Grimshaw, J. and Oxman, A.D., 2012. Audit and feedback: effects on professional practice and healthcare outcomes (review*). The Cochrane Collaboration*. Published by John Wiley & Sons, Ltd.

Joe, G.W., Broome, K. M., Simpson, D. and Rowan-Szal, G. A., 2007, Counselor perceptions of organizational factors and innovations training experiences. *Journal of Substance Abuse Treatment*, 33(2), 171–182.

Jones, G.R., 2007. *Organizational Theory, Design, and Change*. Prentice Hall: New Jersey.

Kanji, G.K., 1996, Implementation and pitfalls of total quality management. *Total Quality Management*, 7(3), 331–343.

Kember, D., Leung, D. and Kwan, K., 2002, Does the use of student feedback questionnaires improve the overall quality of teaching? *Assessment and Evaluation in Higher Education*, 27, 411–425.

Kluger, A.N. and DeNisi, A., 1996, Effects of feedback intervention on performance: a historical review, a meta-analysis, and a preliminary feedback intervention theory. *Psychological Bulletin*, 119(2), 254–284.

KNMG e.a., 2002. *De arts van straks. Een nieuw medischopleidings continuüm [Tomorrow's doctor. A New Educational Continuüm]*. KNMG, Utrecht.

Lange, K. and Baillie, C., 2008. Exploring graduate student learning in applied science and student-supervisor relationships: views of supervisors and their students. *Engineering Education,* 3, 1–14.

Lombarts, M.J.M.H., Arah, O.A., Busch, O.R.C. and Heineman, M.J., 2010. Meten en verbeteren van opleiderskwaliteiten van klinischopleiders met het SETQ-systeem [Using the SETQ system to evaluate and improve teaching qualities of clinical teachers]. *Nederlands Tijdschriftvoor Geneeskunde,* 154, A1222.

McConnell, C. R., 1992. The exit interview: locking the barn door. *Health Care Supervision,* 11(2), 1–10.

Miller, A. and Archer, J., 2010. Impact of workplace-based assessment on doctors' education and performance: a systematic review. *BMJ,* 341, c5064.

Govaerts, M.J.B., Van derVleuten, C.P.M., Schuwirth, L.T.W. and Muijtjens, A.M.M., 2005. The use of observational diaries in in-training evaluation: student perceptions. *Advances in Health Sciences Education,* 10, 171–188.

Murray, J., 2012. 'Cybernetic principles of learning', in N.M. Seel ed., *Encyclopedia of the Sciences of Learning,* Springer US: Boston MA, pp. 902–904, viewed 27 September 2013 from: http://download.springer.com.proxy.library. uu.nl/static/pdf/48/prt%253A978-1-4419-1428-6%252F3.pdf?auth66=1380 189983_1b4762591e0aa0e56f19c79145bcb46f&ext=.pdf

Norcini, J. and Burch, V., 2007. Workplace-based assessment as an educational tool: AMEE Guide No.31. *Medical Teacher,* 29(9), 855–871.

Owlia, M.S. and Aspinwall, E.M., 1997, TQM in higher education – a review. *International Journal of Quality & Reliability Management,* 14(5), 527–543.

Prince, K.J.A.H., Boshuizen, H.P.A., Van der Vleuten, C.P.M. and Scherpbier, A.J.J.A., 2005. Students' opinions about their preparation for clinical practice, *Medical Education,* 37, 704–713.

Roff, S., McAleer, S. and Skinner, A., 2005. Development and validation of an instrument to measure the postgraduate clinical learning and teaching educational environment for hospital-based junior doctors in the UK. *Medical Teacher,* 27(4), 326–331.

Remmen, R., Denekens, J., Scherpbier, A.J.J.A., Van der Vleuten, C.P.M., Hermann, I., Van Puymbroekck, H. and Bossaert, L., 1998. Evaluation of skills training during clerkships using student focus groups. *Medical Teacher,* 20, 428–432.

Richardson, J.T.E., 2005. Instruments for obtaining student feedback: a review of the literature. *Assessment and Evaluation in Higher Education,* 30, 387–415.

Scheele, F., Teunissen, P., Luijk, S., Van, Heineman, E., Fluit, L., Mulder, H., Meininger, A., Wijnen-Meijer, M., Glas, G., Sluiter, H. and Hummel, T., 2008. Introducing competency-based postgraduate medical education in the Netherlands, *Medical Teacher,* 30(3), 248–253.

Schönrock-Adema, J., Heijne-Penninga, M., Van Hell, E.A. and Cohen-Schotanus, J., 2009. Necessary steps in factor analysis: enhancing validation studies of educational instruments. The PHEEM applied to clerks as an example. *Medical Teacher,* 32, e226–e232.

Spooren, P., Brockx, B. and Mortelmans, D., 2013, On the validity of student evaluation of teaching: the state of the art, *Review of Educational Research,* 83(4), 598–642.

Ten Cate, Th.J., Bleker O.P., Büller H.A. and Scherpbier A.J.J.A., 2003. *Opleiden van medischspecialisten – achtergronden en praktijk [Training of medical specialists – background and practice]*. Bohn Stafleu Van Loghum, Houten.

Van der Hem-Stokroos, H.H., Daelmans, H.E.M., Scherpbier, A.J.J.A., Van der Vleuten, C.P.M., de Vries, H. and Haarman, H.J.Th.M., 2001. How effective is a clerkship as a learning environment? *Medical Teacher,* 23, 608–613.

Van der Hem-Stokroos, H.H., 2005. *The clerkship as a learning environment.* Phd thesis. Amsterdam: VrijeUniversiteit.

Van de Ridder, J.M.M., Stokking K.M., McGaghie, W.C. and Ten Cate, O., 2008. What is feedback in clinical education? *Medical Education*, 42, 89–97.

Van de Ridder, J.M.M., McGaghie, W.C., Ten Cate, O. and Stokking, K.M. Measuring trainee perception of the value of feedback in clinical settings (P-FiCS), under review.

Van der Leeuw, R., Lombarts, K., Heineman, M.J. and Arah, O., 2011. Systematic evaluation of the teaching qualities of obstetrics and gynecology faculty: reliability and validity of the SETQ tools. *PLoS ONE,* 6(5), e19142.

Veloski, J., Boex, J.R., Grasberger, M.J., Evans, A. and Wolfson, D.B., 2006. Systematic review of the literature on assessment, feedback and physicians' clinical performance: BEME Guide No. 7, *Medical Teacher*, 28(2), 117–128.

Webster, J., Flint, A. L. and Courtney, M. D., 2009. A new practice environment measure based on the reality and experiences of nurses' working lives. *Journal of Nursing Management*, 17(1), 38–48.

World Federation of Medical Education, 2003, *Postgraduate Medical Education: WFME global standards for quality improvement.* WFME Office, Copenhagen. Viewed 25 October 2013 from *http://www. wfme.org*

Wijnia, M., 2010. *Leerklimaat van de coschappen in het Albert Schweitzer ziekenhuis [Learning climate of the clerkships in the Albert Schweitzer hospital].* Unpublished master's thesis, Utrecht University.

Zabaleta, F., 2007. The use and misuse of student evaluation of teaching. *Teaching in Higher Education*, 12, 55–76.

Notes

1. The quality indicators also need to cover the regional level but this will not be elaborated here, because it is beyond the scope of this chapter.
2. Also: Train the Trainer course, a programme in which potential trainers are trained. The didactic aspects of training are given a lot of attention.

Approaches to Student Feedback in the Health and Medical Sciences

Chenicheri Sid Nair,
University of Western Australia

Patricie Mertova,
Associates in Higher Education Policy,
Development and Quality

Abstract: This chapter draws on the chapters concerning student feedback in medical and health sciences by contributors from around the world. It summarises the key trends, issues and approaches concerning student feedback within the health and medical science disciplines.

Keywords: Student feedback; health and medical sciences; international perspectives; trends

Introduction

The concept of collecting students' feedback on their experience of teaching and learning is not a new concept and has historical precedent. The merits of collecting student feedback on teaching and learning were first acknowledged in the early 1920s (D'Apollonia & Abrami, 1997; McKeachie, 1990), but the trend started gaining momentum only in the early 1990s (Harvey, 2003). This was a result of many factors, but primarily the internationalisation of higher education and the growing need for access to higher education. With growing massification of higher education, stakeholders became more prominent in assessing the quality of institutional teaching and other services. With this impetus, student feedback started playing a greater role within higher education, and students started having a greater input into design of the classroom environment.

The importance of student experience data is clearly articulated in academic literature (Bennett and Nair, 2010; Marsh and Dunkin, 1992) and it includes:

- student and staff reflection on teaching and learning for the development and improvement of teaching and student learning;
- useful research data to underpin further design and improvements to units, courses, curriculum and teaching and services;
- a measure of effectiveness of the learning and teaching environments that may be used in administrative decision-making, e.g. performance management and development appraisal, resource funding;
- a source of useful information for current and potential students in the selection of units and courses and possibly the institution; and
- a measure for judging quality of units and courses which is increasingly becoming tied into external funding formulas.

The academic literature on student experience is extensive. The research suggests that student experience encompasses all aspects of the university experienced by an individual student including the classroom environment and all aspects of engagement in the student life cycle (Coates, 2006; Harvey 2006; Krause, Harley, James, & Mcinnis, 2005; Nair, Patil, & Mertova, 2011).

Student evaluations have no doubt gained a place in national and institutional quality assurance frameworks in higher education to measure the student experience (Shah & Nair, 2012). Institutions are increasingly using student feedback results in course and programme reviews, course accreditations, and in reviewing course quality and viability (Tucker, in press).

With this increasing emphasis on stakeholder feedback, the authors of this book, Nair and Mertova, set out on a quest to fill the void in the academic literature, particularly within individual disciplines, and the discussions on the topic in higher education. This book is the final one in the series on student feedback in various disciplines, with contributions by academics and practitioners on utilising student feedback across the globe. This book specifically addresses practices in the medical and health sciences.

Key trends, issues, and approaches

What transpires from reading the chapters is that student voice has clearly been perceived as a critical factor in assessing and maintaining the quality of health and medical science education. With student voice having a significant place within programmes worldwide, some broad commonalities appear across the various chapters. These commonalities concern four key factors that dominate the student voice in the medical and health science disciplines. The authors of this chapter perceive these factors as emerging trends, issues, and approaches and they are the following:

Factor 1 – Built-in requirement

The chapters clearly articulate that the discipline considers the student voice to be critical in training of medical and health science graduates. What the chapters reveal is that no matter where medical education is taking place, in a developed or third world country, the teaching approaches utilise feedback as a developmental tool to enhance both the teaching and the learning experience. All contributors agree on the significance of reviewing student feedback to enable preparing actions plans and monitoring the changes implemented to ensure that these have been effective in enhancing teaching and learning.

Factor 2 – Tools of the trade

For student feedback to be effective, it is essential to have a number of tools to enable evaluation for different purposes. Teacher and unit evaluations have been discussed in all the chapters. Some chapters also discussed programme evaluations. The chapters have drawn attention to the broad range of channels by which students can provide feedback in the quality cycle and that these channels are by no means uniform within the medical and health science disciplines across the higher education sector nationally. Also, even the extent to which utilising student feedback is established within individual higher education systems varies.

Factor 3 – Qualitative and quantitative tools

A noticeable trend in many of the chapters is the feedback tool design. There is clear recognition that both the quantitative and qualitative components play a critical part in achieving a total picture of perceptions and needs. However, the apparent emphasis in the medical and health science is on the qualitative feedback provided.

Factor 4 – Cultural differences

Chapters 3 and 4 clearly point out that cultural differences play an important role in getting a clear picture of the teaching and learning environment. Chapter 4 (Thai experience), for instance, emphasises the respect of the young towards their elders, which creates resistance to disagreeing with teachers. This factor alone could inhibit free expression of opinions and thus be an impediment to a successful feedback system. Though this is challenging, the system has set up an effective form of gaining student feedback to enhance the learning process, with many academics seeking feedback to improve their teaching as well.

Concluding remarks

Although many of the factors discussed in this book appear in the medical and health sciences contexts, a review of the research literature has shown no difference in student feedback, developments, and actions in other disciplines (Nair & Mertova, 2013). What is more prominent in the medical and health sciences contexts is a greater consistency in the application of student voice to enhance teaching and learning and the recognition of qualitative comments in gaining a deeper understanding of student experience.

This final book in the series adds further to the debate that it is important to contextualise student feedback within a particular discipline and its specifics. Although this debate will continue, especially if one looks at teacher evaluations and item structure, the international contributions in this book suggest that the issues, trends, and approaches faced in understanding and improving as a result of student feedback remain almost identical, and this is reflected in the earlier three publications by the authors (Nair & Mertova, 2013; Nair, Patil, & Mertova, 2012). Similarly to the previous books within the series, the last book suggests that although there are mechanisms developed, the enthusiasm with which institutions across systems embrace student voice for change varies. Whatever the arguments against the future of student voice may be, what is clear is that it forms a part of any effective quality system that values enhancing teaching and learning.

References

Bennett, L. & Nair, C.S. (2010). A recipe for effective participation rates for web-based surveys. *Assessment and Evaluation Journal*, 35(4), 357–366.

Coates, H. (2006). *Student Engagement in Campus-based and Online Education: University Connections.* Taylor & Francis, London, UK.

D'Apollonia, S., & Abrami, P. (1997). Navigating student ratings instructions. *American Psychologist*, 52(11), 1198–1208.

Harvey, L. (2006). Impact of quality assurance: overview of a discussion between representatives of external quality assurance agencies. *Quality in Higher Education*, 12(3), 287–290.

Harvey, L. (2003). Student feedback [1]. *Quality in Higher Education*, 9(1), 3–20. doi: 10.1080/13538320308164.

Krause, K.-L., Hartley, R., James, R., & McInnis, C. (2005). The first year experience in Australian universities: findings from a decade of national studies. Centre for the Study of Higher Education University of Melbourne, Melbourne.

Marsh, H. W. & Dunkin, M. J. (1992). Students' evaluations of university teaching: a multidimensional perspective. In J. C. Smart (Ed.) *Higher Education: Handbook of Theory and Research, Volume 8.* Agathon Press, New York.

McKeachie, W. (1990). Research on college teaching. The historical background. *Journal of Education Psychology*, 82(2), 189–200.

Nair, C.S. and Mertova, P. (2013). *Enhancing Learning and Teaching through Student Feedback in Social Sciences.* Woodhead Publishing: Cambridge, UK.

Nair, C.S., Patil, A. and Mertova, P. (2012). *Enhancing Learning and Teaching through Student Feedback in Engineering.* Woodhead Publishing: Cambridge, UK.

Nair, C. S., Patil, A. and Mertova, P. (2011). Enhancing the quality of engineering education by utilising student feedback, *European Journal of Engineering Education*, 36(1), 3–12.

Shah, M. (2013). The prominence of student voice in tertiary education. In Shah, M. & Nair. C. S. (Eds) *Enhancing Student Feedback and Improvement Systems in Tertiary Education, Commission of Academic Accreditation (CAA), Quality Series, UAE.*

Shah, M. & Nair, C. S. (2012). The changing nature of teaching and unit evaluations in Australian universities. *Quality Assurance in Education, 20(3)*, 274–288.

Tucker, B. (in press). Student evaluation to improve the student learning experience: an Australian university case study. *Educational Research and Evaluation.*